View from the Church tower about 1880, before the Old Vicarage was built

Madron's Story

Written and compiled by Michael Dundrow
Researched by Margaret Dundrow and Ann Jenkin
Photography by Doug Davies

Michael Dundrow

Margaret Dundrow

Bossiney Books · Launceston

Thanks are due to the following, whose donations made this book possible:

Betty Berryman
Mr and Mrs W W Cock
Mr and Mrs D Davies
Mr and Mrs B Edwards
Mrs C Ede
Mr and Mrs T Furlong
Mrs W Le Grice
Mr and Mrs B King
Mr and Mrs D Luddlcoat
Madron Old Cornwall Society

Madron Parish Council
Madron Women's Institute
Mr and Mrs D Mann
Mr and Mrs C Pollard
Mr G Quinn
Mrs C Smart
Mrs J Smith
Mrs P Snow
Mrs J Starnes
Mrs R White

First published 2001 by
Bossiney Books, Langore, Launceston, Cornwall PL15 8LD

ISBN 1-899383-48-4

The cover photograph shows Doreen King (left) and Pat Snow (Bardic name Myrgh Essa) at the Cornish Gorsedd, Hayle, 1999.

Printed and bound by Image Design & Print Limited, Bodmin, Cornwall PL31 1EP

Some books consulted

Prehistoric Cornwall – The Ceremonial Monuments by John Barnatt (Turnstone Press, 1982)
Cornish Archaeology, No. 33, 1994
Ancient & Holy Wells by A Quiller Couch
Cornwall and its People by AK Hamilton Jenkin (JM Dent, 1945; David & Charles Reprints, 1970)
Stone Crosses in West Penwith by Andrew Langdon (Federation of Old Cornwall Societies, 1997)
The History of the Town and Borough of Penzance by PAS Pool (Corporation of Penzance, 1974)
'A Century for Madron' and 'History of Madron'(unpublished) by Reverend FW Warnes
Face the Music by Harry Woodhouse (Cornish Hillside Publications, 1997)

Acknowledgements

The author and publishers would like to thank the following contributors:

Miss M Christopher: Bell ringers
Mr J Cock: Madron at war
Mr W W Cock: Chapel, Cricket
Mrs S Dann: Handbell ringers
Mr A Davenport: Football
Mr D Davies: Scouting, Guise dancing
Mr A Figg: Cub scouts
Mr L Green: Madron Young Farmers Club, Bossullow
Reverend P Horder: slides of Trengwainton Garden
Mrs A Jenkin: Madron Young Farmers Club, Farming in Madron
Mr B King: photographic records and maps
Mrs W Le Grice: photograph of her husband and herself at Trereife (page 60)
Mr G Quinn: The playing field
Mrs Z Roberts: photograph, 'Hay Baling Interlude' (page 118)
Reverend J Robertshaw: access to parish registers
Mr J Rowe: Scouting
Mrs T Rowe: St Maddern's School today
Mr B Sparrow: The Western Hunt
Mrs J Starnes: tape recordings of interview with Louie Nicholls
Mrs C Summers: Girl guiding
Mr H Thomas: Boswarthen
Miss K Toms & Miss G Goldstone: Nursing in Madron
Mrs S Westren: Handbell ringers
The Cornishman: use of photographs and extracts
The West Briton: use of extracts
The Western Morning News: use of photographs
Madron Old Cornwall Society: use of records
Madron WI: use of scrap books

and many others in and out of the parish who have helped with information and photographs to make this account as accurate as possible. Our thanks are also due to Peter Scrase for reading the manuscript and for making many valuable suggestions.

We are also grateful to the following sources of information:

Cornwall Record Office, including reproduction of documents on page 30 (P133/7/4) and page 31 (X272/-47)
Madron Old Cornwall Society Records
Madron WI Minute Books & Scrapbooks
Parish Church Records and Magazines
Article on Madron Workhouse by Frank Ruhrmund
'Notes on the History of Madron, Morvah & Penzance', Canon Jennings, 1936
The author is indebted for much of the information on Ding Dong to an article by

C B Orchard in *Cornish Magazine* dated September 1967.

Contents

Introduction

I am very glad to have been asked to write a short introduction to *Madron's Story*, each of whose many contributors must be congratulated for their dedication and immense hard work.

I myself came to West Cornwall sixty years ago and, having been born and brought up near London, it was a complete revelation to me. I soon realised that those of us who lived at Trereife belonged to the parish of Madron which stretches down to the sea one way and onto the wide open moors the other way. Madron village in particular made a big impression upon me – there was a feeling of antiquity and security – and in no time at all I began to feel a real affinity with it. I discovered all its interesting parts and surroundings, and loved to walk down the long lane to the Baptistry, passing on the way Madron Wishing Well. The Baptistry is a magical place as indeed is the Wishing Well, which has cemented romance for many young Madron couples.

The longer I lived in the parish, the more I felt I belonged to it. In the early days there was so much village life and all sorts of activities, ranging from Feast Week and the Women's Institute May Revels to the Feast Concert in which most Madron people took part. Every year on Feast Sunday we would sing the long hymn which features Madron parish and I don't think anybody actually knew a great deal about St Maddern who seemed a shadowy figure, possibly coming from Ireland.

But that really is unimportant. What is important is that the known, documented history is now preserved for posterity in *Madron's Story* thanks to a committed group of people each of whom, like me, has experienced the parish at close hand. Read for yourselves all they have lovingly written, and be prepared for some surprises along the way!

Wilmay Le Grice, 2001

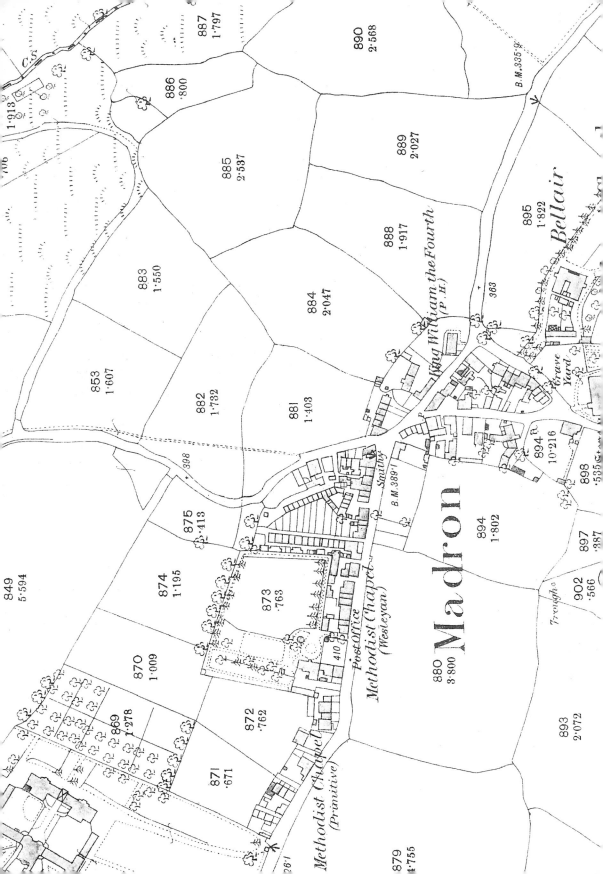

Preface

In the millennium year 2000 a Festival of Flowers, including displays of historical artefacts, took place in Madron Church to help raise funds for floor repairs. All village groups contributed and provided a wealth of material – parish and church records; background to May Day celebrations, 'Crying the neck' and the Midsummer Bonfire; captivating old photographs capturing a century of life in and around Madron; handbells; robes... The festival was so successful that requests were made for a more permanent record of Madron's past – whence this book has arisen.

Although we have attempted to cover as many aspects of Madron's distant and more recent history as possible, we are very conscious that a degree of failure is inevitable – no single volume of this type can be exhaustive in the treatment of its subject and there are doubtless many features of Madron's story that could have whole books written about them. We took the hard decision to tailor our accounts to practical limitations of time and available space. Nevertheless we feel that the fascinating overall picture of Madron's life which has emerged during our research will be immensely satisfying for our readers.

It goes without saying that we have tried to be accurate in the things we recount. We have cross-checked and taken advice and verified as much as we can. Memory can, however, play tricks and in the end we can only beg our readers' indulgence for any remaining errors and omissions.

Opposite: An Ordnance Survey map of 1878, drawn at 1:2500 scale

Having fallen during a storm in 1815, Lanyon Quoit was re-erected with only three supports instead of the original four. Before that the great cap-stone, weighing 13.5 tonnes, stood about 2.5 metres clear of the ground – high enough for a horse and rider to pass beneath

Only the capstone and one support remain of West Lanyon Quoit. It was discovered in 1790 when 100 cartloads of good soil were removed from the mound which covered it. Human bones were found beneath it at that time

Prehistory in Madron

This corner of West Penwith which we know today as Madron parish is old, extremely old in terms of human occupation and activity.

Lanyon Quoit (locally 'Cromlech'), Mulfra Quoit and West Lanyon Quoit are probably the oldest of Madron's many prehistoric remains, with Chûn Quoit just over the border in Morvah. They were built with simple stone tools as tombs around 5000 years ago, and even now are still impressive monuments.

Madron also has a number of menhirs, or longstones, scattered about the parish. They form a major part of the prehistoric picture of West Penwith which

Mulfra Quoit is located near the summit of Mulfra Hill. Its capstone has slipped off and rests against two uprights. Like all the chambered tombs, it was covered in earth, though possibly not completely, to form a large circular barrow

Boskednan stone circle, also known as 'the Nine Maidens', is a fascinating example of a type of monument for which nobody knows the original purpose. Theories range from astronomical calendars to tribal ceremonial centres, often with ley line overtones

has a greater density of menhirs per square mile than any other region of Britain. The function of these isolated stones, most of them from the Bronze Age, so far defies clear explanation. Burials are sometimes associated with them, as at Trye and Trewern, but often nothing is found. Were they erected as boundary markers or as guide posts, or to denote meeting places, or did they play a part in religious rituals? We can only conjecture.

Chûn Castle on the border with Morvah is a splendid Iron Age hilltop fort dating from about 300 BC. Pieces of tin slag found there show that the inhabitants knew how to smelt tin and that the local source of the ore brought traders to the area. Records from Roman writers show that landings were made along

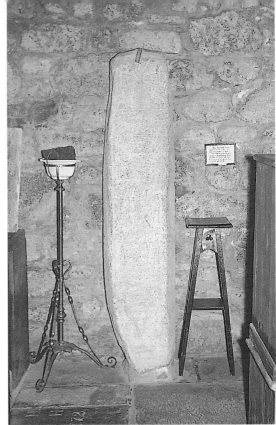

Left: The most famous menhir in Madron is Mên Scryfa – the written stone. The words chiselled into it appear to say 'To Rialbran, son of Cunoval' who was possibly a local chief during the post-Roman period

Right: It is interesting that this menhir was actually built into the wall of the parish church, and was not recognised until 1936. Like Mên Scryfa, it was inscribed early in the Christian era

Chûn Castle was originally defended by two massive drystone ramparts and deep ditches

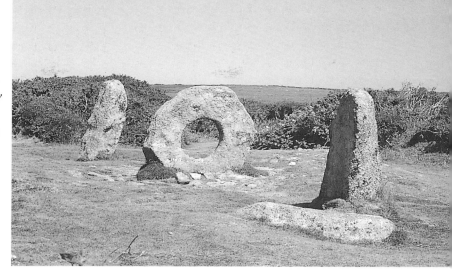

This is the Mên-an-Tol, another mystery to archaeologists. It is sometimes known as 'the Crick Stone' because years ago a supposed cure for childhood rickets was to crawl through the hole 'nine times against the sun'

Long before the present village was thought of, a farming community tilled small square fields and tended cattle at Chysauster, and in times of trouble took refuge in the fort on the hill above

the coast, probably at St Michael's Mount. Gold bracelets discovered nearby in the early 1900s are now in the British and Truro Museums.

Below Chûn Castle at Bossullow, Trehyllys, are the remains of a small settlement which may, like Chysauster, be connected with its neighbouring fort.

Chysauster – the famous collection of Iron Age houses below the hill fort at Castle-an-Dinas – is, with perhaps Trehyllys, the earliest village site in Madron parish. Today, thanks to excavation, we can follow the layout of the houses along the street, and imagine doors where the post holes are, water channels and garden areas and, half closing our eyes, see in our mind's eye our ancient village ancestors going about their daily lives.

11

The Baptistry

Madron Well and Baptistry

Cornwall has many holy wells, but none is more famous than Madron Well which is reputed never to run dry. The wells' origins lie in pre-Christian customs of honouring spirits who were thought to reside in them and offering gifts of precious metallic objects, such as axe heads and brooches, in the hope they would continue magically to provide life-giving water from below ground.

When St Maddern came this way to convert the heathen Cornish in probably the 5th or 6th century, he was keen to turn such pagan practices to the profit of Christianity.

He built a baptistry, a forerunner of the present building, over the stream nearby and, no doubt after powerful preaching, baptized his converts on the spot.

This mixture of Christian and pagan beliefs is well captured by Joan Tregenza in the Eden Philpott's novel of the same name. Speaking of the rags 'tored off a petticoat or some sich thing' by mothers after dipping their babies naked in the brook, she says, 'They hanged 'em up around about on the thorn bushes to shaw as they'd 'a' done more for the good saint if they'd had the power. An' theer's another marvellous thing as washin' in thicky waters done, it kep' the fairies off – the bad fairies I mean, 'cause there'm good an' bad piskies, same as good an' bad men folks.'

Nowadays the hallmark of Madron Well is the pieces of rag, ribbon, etc tied to twigs that have been left by visitors making special wishes at the site. But it is not so long ago, and certainly within living memory, that the young people of the village made a very small cross for the same purpose, using a pin and a rush. They dropped their pin into the crystal clear water and made a wish. As the bubbles rose, they counted them and were able to calculate the precise time when the wish would be granted.

Someone once wrily commented, 'Beside the sanctities and Christian certainties of the ancient Baptistry, how frivolous and puerile and superstitious seem the May-tide Pin and Rush custom of Madron's other antiquity – the Wishing Well.'

Traditionally, however, the well was most sought after for its healing properties. 'Here,' says AK Hamilton Jenkin in *Cornwall & its People* (David & Charles, 1970, p. 309), 'on the first three Wednesdays in May, children afflicted with shingles, wildfire, tetters and other skin complaints were plunged through the waters three times against the sun, being afterwards carried nine times around the spring going from east to west, or with the sun.'

Miraculous cures at Madron Well go back centuries, but not many are so well attested as the healing of John Trelille who was baptized at Madron on 18 November 1610. No less a person than Bishop Hall of Exeter on a visit in 1640 saw for himself, along with hundreds of Trelille's neighbours, 'this man that for 16 years together was fain to walk upon his hands by reason of the close contraction of the sinews of his legs – on being told in a dream to wash himself three times in the well, was suddenly so restored to his limbs that I saw him able to walk and get his maintenance' (as quoted by Canon Jennings in 'Notes on Madron, Morvah & Penzance' from Quiller Couch's *Ancient & Holy Wells of Cornwall*, p.126).

We must not forget that the stream flowing from Madron Well supplied Churchtown with its water for centuries. According to Canon Jennings until 1899, when it was piped, water ran in an open leat across the fields. This amazing spring was also a main supplier of water to Penzance until 1830. It ran down the hill into a reservoir at the top of Causewayhead and for many years powered the fountains in Morrab Gardens.

The Baptistry altar

Cross in the churchyard, possibly a grave marker

Boswarthen Cross, still at its original site but badly fractured in the 1860s

Stone crosses

Among Madron's many fascinating antiquities must be included the eight stone or wayside crosses that are dotted about the present day civil parish (there are fourteen crosses in the older and larger ecclesiastical parish which included Penzance and part of Newlyn).

With perhaps one exception, their main purpose was to mark the way to the parish church. So they stood at the side of ancient tracks and footpaths running from the churchtown to outlying farms and hamlets. Experts, such as Andrew Langdon in his *Stone Crosses in West Penwith* (Federation of Old Cornwall Societies, 1997), date the wayside crosses from about the 12th century; they were probably put up when the Church's parochial system was being created.

Madron's eight crosses are:

1. The wheelheaded cross two metres to the west of the church tower (until 1896 it had been in a hedge close to the blacksmith's shop). On one face is carved the clothed body of Christ. The holes drilled into it, probably by miners' rock drills, were perhaps a type of apprentices' vandalism.

Boscathnoe Cross

2. Also in the churchyard, by the path near the south porch, is a small cross which, by its geometric design, may be of a later date than the others. It was possibly a grave marker rather than a wayside cross.

3. Boscathnoe Cross is a damaged Latin cross (a plain cross with the lowest arm longer than the other three) standing beside the old path running south from the church.

4. A quarter of a mile east of Buryas Bridge beside the A30 stands Trembath Cross. It is on an old track from Paul Church to Madron and is thought to be *in situ* – in its original position.

5. At a point on the same old track and near the farm of the same name is Parc an Growse Cross. This stone is unusual in not displaying the cross symbol.

6. Tremethick Cross is set up high in a hedge beside the A307 road from Penzance to St Just. It was moved during the19th century from Rose an Beagle in Paul parish and stands now on the same ancient track as the previous two monuments.

7. The wheelheaded Boswarthen Cross was probably set up to guide pilgrims to the nearby holy well and baptistry. It is still *in situ* on its original base, though it was badly fractured some time during the 1860s. One local resident said that when she was young her father used to tell her to walk three times round Boswarthen Cross and spit three times and then 'the devil would not get you'.

Trengwainton Carn Cross

8. Trengwainton Carn Cross, beside an old church footpath from Boswarva across the Carn, has lost its shaft, but is sitting in its original base stone and is thought to be *in situ*.

Madron's patron saint

It is generally agreed that Madron owes its name to its patron saint – though it was 'Maddern' for many years and still is occasionally for locals. But where the saint came from or when, and indeed anything much about his life, is mostly conjecture. Early Celtic Christian legends talk of a St Maddern arriving from Brittany during the 5th century, staying a while in Cornwall, then going on to Ireland before settling in Wales. But the names, spellings and even gender vary between the stories; there is nothing that can be relied upon as hard fact.

Sharing the haziness of those early times in Madron we have, hard by the church, the ancient domain of Landithy – the 'lan' or sacred enclosure of Dithy. Legend has it that Dithy might have been one of the companions of St Ia, patron of St Ives, in the 5th century and that here, close to the present parish church, he may have built his little church. If so he was probably years earlier than Maddern, which might explain why the church is where it is, by Dithy's lan, rather than out by the wishing well.

In any case it is pretty certain that as Canon Doble, late vicar of Wendron and an authority on Cornish saints, said, 'Madron, with its lan or monastery

The banner. It has been in the Church for longer than even the oldest residents can remember

called after a Celtic saint Dithy, its holy well and shrine of St Madron or Madern and its numerous ancient crosses, was once an important Celtic settlement.'

Madron in the Middle Ages

From about AD 600 to AD 1000 nothing is known of the happenings in the parish. It is only after the Norman Conquest of 1066 that we can start to glean information. We learn for example from *Domesday Book* (1087) that Landithy, Trengwainton and Madron Church were part of the manor of Roseworthy in Gwinear and were held before 1066 by Earl Harold. Then on the principle of 'winner takes all' they were seized by the Conqueror himself before being given to his half brother Robert, Earl of Mortain, who was created Earl of Cornwall.

The rest of the parish, which had belonged to the manor of Alwareton (Alverton), also became the property of Robert of Mortain, and on his death in 1097 passed to his son William. He, however (unwisely as it turned out), joined a revolt against the king, was captured in battle, had his eyes put out, his lands and privileges taken away, and died a monk in Bermondsey in 1140.

Reginald de Dunstanville, an illegitimate son of Henry I, became the next Earl of Mortain and of Cornwall. He gave Roseworthy, including Madron, Landithy and Trengwainton, to his sister Rohesia as a wedding present on her marriage to Baron Henry de Pomeroy. The charter dealing with this event, which has survived and is preserved at Tregothnan, home of Lord Falmouth, begins the long written history of Madron.

Their son, Henry de Pomeroy II, also backed the wrong side, and no doubt regretted it dearly. This time it was for Prince John against his brother Richard the Lion Heart, then imprisoned in Austria. Charged with high treason when Richard returned, before he committed suicide as some say, Henry granted Madron to the Knights Hospitaller. He was hoping to deflect the king's wrath, for Richard had learned the value of the Knights of St John on his crusade.

During all this confusion, one Thomas de Chimelly had been appointed in 1203 to the benefice of Madron for life, and it was agreed that the Knights would inherit the benefice after Thomas's death. In 1309 the Knights turned the living of Madron from a rectory to a vicarage, which it has remained ever since. This allowed the rectorial tithe, or tax, to go to the treasury of the Order. (A rector was entitled to all the tithes levied in the parish, whereas a vicar was entitled to only a portion.) The extra income was used for their work in helping pilgrims and building hospitals.

So the property at Landithy became a centre of hospitality for the Knights of St John and a stopping place for all sorts of travellers on the journey from Mousehole (then, according to Canon Jennings, 'the only port on Mount's Bay') into England. Pilgrims and officials would have travelled on foot and by pony, passing up the hill to Paul and along the old track with wayside crosses which still stand, up to Madron where they could rest and find refreshment at Landithy. Madron in those days would have been in close touch with national and international events, its finger on the pulse of medieval life.

This work went on until 1540 when the Order was suppressed and its possessions confiscated by Henry VIII, but in modern times the Order has been revived by royal charter, in the shape of the St John's Ambulance Brigade, and performs sterling work at events across the country.

After the suppression, Queen Elizabeth I granted Landithy to Nicholas Fleming. A memorial to his son Thomas Fleming can be seen in the church. It is interesting to note that, although Landithy passed into other hands, the Fleming family did not die out. In fact, Mollie Fleming Scrase (née Fleming Evans) is a descendant of this same family, a remarkable fact which Canon Hocking recorded in *The Cornishman* in 1949.

Madron Church

13 July 1336 was a red letter day for Madron. The bishop journeyed all the way from Exeter, a long and difficult excursion indeed when roads were mere rutted tracks infested with outlaws. He came to consecrate the new Madron church, or the part that had been erected so far – the south arcade and the chancel with its great altar. We can imagine the fussing and the frenzied preparations for this unprecedented occasion, for Bishop Grandisson didn't travel alone. Oh no! He had with him his two archdeacons, the chancellor of the cathedral plus the Lord Prior of the Knights of St John in London, many clergymen and knights, and a whole multitude of grooms and servants.

We hear nothing untoward about what happened that day, so presumably all went well. In fact Madron probably did not detain the bishop for too long, as he had no less than 14 other churches to consecrate on his summer tour and some serious talking to do at St Buryan to rebellious parishioners!

The church was not actually completed as we see it today, with north aisle, until 1500. Before then, the vicar Benedict Tregos must have spent many a sleepless night sweating with terror after he backed Perkin Warbeck, who landed at Sennen in 1499 claiming to be Richard IV. It probably seemed a good idea at the time to Tregos, but it was a high risk strategy and one which fell apart when Warbeck was captured and suffered the loser's penalty in such a hazardous game.

Luckily for him, Tregos was a wealthy man. By lavishing his money on the church – paying for the north aisle, and arranging for Tudor roses to be placed on a pillar and the king's arms on expensive panelling – he desperately tried to deflect the charge of treason. It worked. Henry VII pardoned him and he died peacefully many years later.

Madron Church is easily the most impressive building in the attractive Churchtown, prominent upon its rocky perch surveying Mount's Bay from over 120 metres up. It can justly lay claim to be one of Cornwall's finest churches, its interior being spacious yet powerful in its proportions and full of the atmosphere and echoes of the past. Unlikely as it may seem now to the casual visitor, Madron was also for a long time the mother church of Penzance. Until the middle of the 19th century the whole of Penzance and half of Newlyn were in the

Above: The Church as it was in the early 19th century, with the old school house on the far left, engraved from a drawing by Miss M U Peters

Below: The Church in the 1990s

The Nelson banner

Mourn for the Brave
the immortal NELSON'S gone,
His last Sea fight is fought
his work of Glory done.

parish of Madron, and until 1870 the mayor and corporation had by law to come in state to Madron on the first Sunday in October to receive holy communion.

These days tradition is upheld in the form of the famous Trafalgar Service and brings great animation to Madron Churchtown. The following note from the Order of Service explains the origins:

'On 21st October 1805 the British Fleet under the command of Vice-Admiral Lord Nelson met the combined French and Spanish fleets which were under the command of Vice-Admiral Pierre Charles Villeneuve. They engaged battle off Cape Trafalgar. The French and Spanish fleets were defeated but Lord Nelson died of his wounds aboard his flagship HMS *Victory*.

'HMS *Pickle*, under the command of Lieut. Lapenotière, set sail immediately for Falmouth, to carry the news of the victory and of Lord Nelson's death. On

The Parade, possibly in 1947

the way, HMS *Pickle* encountered a fishing vessel from Penzance and passed the news to her crew. So it was that the first news of Nelson's death was announced from the Assembly Rooms (now part of the Union Hotel) in Penzance on 4th November 1805.

'A procession, headed by the Mayor of Penzance, made its way to Madron Parish Church (as the Mother Church of Penzance) where a memorial service was held and the Nelson Banner was paraded for the first time.'

The verse on the banner reads:

> Mourn for the Brave, the immortal Nelson's gone,
> His last Sea fight is fought, his work of Glory done.

The annual commemoration of Nelson's death was begun on 27 October 1946 by the Reverend (later Canon) Michael Hocking, vicar of Madron and a former naval chaplain. So many wished to attend that the service had to be relayed outside the church to those who could not get in. The captain of HMS *Wizard*, which was lying in Mount's Bay, invited the choirboys on board for a tour.

Taking the Salute at Landithy Hall

Today the event takes place on the Sunday nearest to 21 October, with civic dignitaries and naval personnel past and present marching through the village. A band plays, there is the taking of salutes, and everyone – including the general public – converges on Madron to honour England's most popular hero.

Parish registers

These invaluable, if brief, records of the essential milestones in the lives of local people, from the humble cottager to the wealthy and privileged, are a treasure chest of village information, one for which posterity owes a debt of gratitude to our churches for providing.

The registers for Madron are in an excellent state of preservation. They begin in 1577 for marriages and burials, and in 1592 for baptisms, earlier pages for baptisms being inexplicably lost. Dipping into them gives us glimpses as through a tiny, clouded window of the customs and events of centuries past. A ban on marriages in Lent, for example, seems to have been strictly adhered to during the universally observed period of fasting and heightened piety running

23

up to Good Friday. Then again, no records at all were kept for 1595, the year the Spaniards landed and attacked Paul, Mousehole, Newlyn and Penzance. The effect on the whole district of the shooting, fires and roar of cannon, together with wildfire rumour, must have been traumatic and long lasting.

Immorality in the 17th century left only slight traces of its existence in the village. In all there are about 60 entries of illegitimate children during a period of 100 years or so, marked in the registers by *spur* (short for 'spurious') against certain names. Plagues struck the village on more than one occasion. In 1578, for example, whole families were swept away during a six-month period:

Burials 1578

Julye 8.	Thomas, son of William Hawke
Julye 8.	Radigonn, daughter of William Hawke
Julye 8.	Jane, daughter of William Hawke
Julye 25.	William Hawke
Julye 25.	Nicholas, son of John Goodale
Aug. 6.	William, son of John Goodale
Aug.10.	John, son of John Goodale
Aug.10.	Christian, wife of John Goodale
Aug.10.	Johnathan, son of John Goodale

In total 150 people were buried in this same period, whereas the normal burial rate was less than three a month.

The following selected entries from the registers give a flavour of the type of information given over the years and show a rich variety of names, many of which still occur in and around Madron.

Marriages

1577 September 20th   Were married Hughe Cooke of Pawle and Agnes the daughter of John Legowe.

1661 March 5th   John Hicks, gent, and Katherine daughter of John Cowling of Trengwainton, gent.

1703 December 29th   John Davy and Margaret Cock, both of Maddern.

1721 October 13th   John Thomas of Germo and Catherine Gabriel of this parish.

1723 December 1st   Justinian Bonetto and Joan Wallish, both of this parish.

1730 February 2nd   Martin Angwin of this parish and Constance Eddy of the parish of Zennor.

1731 October 24th   Robert Stephens of St. Berion and Mary Nicholas of this parish.

1732 June 30th   Mr John Searle of the Island of St. Mary's in Scilly and Mrs
Blanche Tregurtha of Penzance by licence dated 15th June.

1733 April 3rd   Stephen Dale of this parish and Grace Harvey of the parish of
Zennor.

Baptisms

The first records are for 1592:

September 24th was baptized Joane, the daughter of John Cornish.

November 5th was baptized Joane, the daughter of John Martyn.

1593, January 21st was baptized John, the sonne of William Maderne.

1594, April 7th,   Richard, son of Raphe Lanyon.

1606, January 12th,   James, son of William Bone.

1606, July 27th,   John, son of Richard Nickles [Nicholls].

1614, February 16th,   Elizabeth, daughter of Arthur Edye [Eddy].

1623, April 24th,   Alice, daughter of Robert Trewern.

1634, October 13th,   Richard, son of William Treneere.

1713, September 14th,   Mary, daughter of William Bramwell of Penzance.

1714, March 1st,   Margret, daughter of William Cock of Penzance.

1714, August 22nd,   Samuel, the son of Samuel Dale of Maddern.

1715, September 19th,   John the son of Willam Pollard of Madron.

1716, June 22nd,   Ann, the daughter of Francis Lanyon of Penzance.

1724, February 9th,   Henry, son of Henry Williams (Shoemaker)

1724, February 13th,   Henry, son of Henry Williams (Fisherman).

1726, September 21st,   Richard, son of Richard Keate by his late wife's sister.

1727, April 3rd,   John, son, Elizabeth daughter of Thomas Rodda of
Tremethack.

Burials 'Beginninge in Anno 1577'

Maye 20,   was buryed John Fynny the sonne of Richard Fynnie.

August 21,   was buryed William Trewern.

1578, March 3,   was buryed John, the sonne of Nicholas Kinge.

July 19,   Henrie, son of Richard Maderne.

September 12th,   William, son of John Martin.

1680, April 29,   Robert Polard of ye P[ar]ish of Klovelly in ye County of
Devon, marinor.

1709, March 26th,   Robert Tr'thal of Maddern.

1730, June 25th,   Richard son of Richard Keate by his late wife's sister.

It is interesting to note that immediately after the plague visitation of 1647, a
year in which 217 parishioners were buried, including the vicar John Keate, the
number of marriages ran at almost treble the normal rate and baptisms more

than doubled in this seemingly rapid response to disaster. A similar pattern emerges in the 18th century: deaths were unusually high in 1723, 1730, 1736, 1743, 1755, 1761, 1766-67, 1779-80, 1788-89 and 1792. Also in 1802, 1810-12, 1823, 1832, 1834 and 1837. In almost every case the number of marriages greatly increased in the following year and baptisms in the year after that. Ages among 114 registered Madron marriages at this time averaged 25 years for men and 24 for women.

In addition to the registers themselves, the parish preserved other records, for example this census return signed by the vicar and churchwardens:

Complete Census Return, Maddern parish Aprill 5th 1676

1st   We suppose there may be in the Parish of Maddern and town of Penzance… at least a thousand inhabitants.

2nd   We know None popish recusant among yᵉ sayd inhabitants, and believe there are none such.

3rd   The dissenters and such as obstinately refuse and absent themselves from yᵉ communion of yᵉ Church of England at such times as by law they are commanded – of this sort we know of but only one man.

There are no other local records of the population of Madron or Penzance prior to the census of 1801. The next table shows figures for the earlier part of the 19th century:

	Population				Increase		
	1801	1811	1821	1831	1811	1821	1831
Madron	1564	1817	2011	2058	253	194	47
Penzance	3382	4022	5224	6563	640	1202	1339
Total	4946	5839	7235	8621	893	1396	1386

In 1831 the census records:
'Houses in Madron, Inhabited 377, uninhabited 35. Total 412.
5 houses were built in Madron in 1831.
Males in Madron's population 978, females 1080, total 2058.
Males above age 20, 492, females ditto, 485.'

The changing Church

The situation concerning pastoral care by the Church has had a period of uncertainty in recent years. Reverend Gilbert came as priest-in-charge in 1981, looking after St Thomas', Heamoor, Madron and Morvah. Church services were rearranged to satisfy parishioners, but at a Church Council meeting it was noted that Madron was becoming more urban. Changes were in the air. In 1984 Morvah (then part of the parish) was moved and joined with Pendeen; Bone Valley and Mulfra with Gulval. This was the end of an era, a link which had lasted 594 years since 1390 when Roger Melleder became the first incumbent of Madron with Morvah.

When Reverend Gilbert accepted an appointment to the Church of King Charles the Martyr at Falmouth, he referred in his farewell letter to 'many quiet changes' which had occurred at Madron, mainly in connection with boundary changes. He warned that the greater part of Treneere and Pendennis estates and Chyandour would move from Madron to the parish of St John the Baptist, Penzance. This duly took effect in 1986, leaving one stipendiary priest in charge at Madron.

Churchyard reconstruction

Madron churchyard saw drastic changes in the early 19th century. By 1820, after centuries of interments, the traditional circular God's Acre was rapidly becoming full, so it was decided to extend it on the north side.

This was the only practical solution, the other sides being ringed about by roads and the school. Even so, it turned out to be a difficult and expensive process, the main points of which included: diverting the stream from Madron Well, which ran in an open leat across the new ground; demolishing a cottage, which also stood there, and compensating the leaseholder; and moving tons of earth to a depth of six feet to bring it up to the general level.

With all the usual ample fees for licences and lawyers, the burden for the parish was considerable and, with long delays over getting the bishop out from Exeter, the new burial ground was not consecrated for use until 1828.

Among the expenses entries preserved in the churchwarden's accounts are the following items:

'Gunpowder and quills for blasting rocks 4s. 6d.
Richard Jenkin for taking down hedge against road, nine days, 13s. 6d.
Taking down old house on new churchyard, £1 10s. 0d.
Geo. Pawley, building 71 perch of wall [390 yards] £7 2s. 0d.
For moving earth from churchtown lane to fill new churchyard level with old, 16 days, £5 14s. 0d.
Alex Berryman for engraving stone to record addition to graveyard £1 11s. 6d.
[this stone is now at the north-east corner of the churchyard]'
Much later – six years in fact – 'cake and wine for Bishop's refreshment 12s. 0d.'

The Scobell Armstrong monument

The total cost of the whole reconstruction venture was £369 11s. 6d.

There are several interesting features in the churchyard, including the Trereife vault for the Le Grice family and the Scobell Armstrongs of Nancealverne. The very large granite mausoleum which dominates the eastern side was erected by the Rose Price family in 1828. They lived at Trengwainton, having acquired their fortune from sugar plantations in Jamaica. The Rose Price four-in-hand carriage was to be seen driving through the neighbourhood complete with Jamaicans as bewigged and liveried postillions. (In Heamoor, Jamaica Place and Jamaica Terrace bear witness to this West Indian connection, the cottages having been built, it is said, for housing Rose Price's workmen.)

It seems rather a shame that by 1878 the churchyard was again full and had to be closed, this time for good. The church side of Madron cemetery on the edge of the village was consecrated the following year by Dr Benson, the first bishop of the new see of Truro.

Madron Church in the 1870s, showing the old box pews

Church restoration

After the churchyard had received its extension in the 1820s, it was not long before the church interior was looked at with a rigorous upgrading in mind.

In the past Madron Church's interior was limewashed every other year and whitewashed occasionally, making the walls and pillars stark white. There was no form of heating or lighting, so there was no evening service. As for seating, the various local landowners and other persons of substance paid to have their own pews built. These were large box-type constructions to contain their families, and also other lesser pews for their servants. The following list for 1836-37 shows who had pews and how much they cost to repair.

		£	s.	d.
1836	Sir Rose Price's executors for Poltegan pew	2	5	0
	F. Paynter for Alverne pew	5	0	0
	Rev. C.V. Le Grice for Tregavara pew		10	6
	T. Bolitho for Landithy pew	4	0	0
1837	Rev. T. Pascoe for Laregan pew	2	0	0
	R. Richards for Boswarthen pew		14	0
	John Richards for Lower Landithy pew	2	0	0

MADRON CHURCH BUILDING COMMITTEE,

In Account with T. B. BOLITHO, Treasurer.

Dr.

PAYMENTS.

From December, 1885, to April, 1889.

	£	s.	d.
To paid Mr. Burch, for faculty	6	6	0
" Mr. J. D. Sedding, Architect's Fees, Travelling Expenses, &c.	229	1	0
" Mr. R. Stanlake and the Trustee of his Estate in Bankruptcy, in full settlement of all amounts due on Contract, and for extras	1925	4	6
" Mr. J. Leggo, his Salary as Clerk of the Works......	64	5	0
" Mr. G. Gendall for New Door, and small bills for sundry alterations	12	10	0
" Sundry small bills, and petty disbursements per Rev. F. Tonkin......	21	8	0
" Messrs. Longdon & Co., for Ironwork, including Heating Apparatus, Gates, &c., &c.	218	4	5
" Messrs. Trask for Chancel Pavement, Choir Stalls, Screen, Carving, &c.	295	0	0
	£2771	18	11

1889.
April 8. To above Balance (deficiency) 592 4 9

Cr.

RECEIPTS.

	£	s.	d.
By received Subscriptions and sundry Contributions as per list, including proceeds of Bazaar, &c.	2129	14	2
" Grant from Church Building Society ,,	50	0	0
Balance......	592	4	9
	£2771	18	11

The accounts for the reconstruction, preserved in the Cornwall Record Office, show something of the work undertaken. The main contractor seems to have been overtaken by bankruptcy during the course of the work

Mrs Thompson for Bosiljack pew	3	0	0
Rev. C.V. Le Grice for 2 pews S. Aisle	6	0	0
R. Richards for Trengwainton pew	3	0	0
S. Borlase for pew in N. Aisle	2	4	0
H.P. Tremenheere, Boscathnoe pew in N. Aisle	2	0	0
Capt. Giddy for Poltair pew	2	0	0
Wm. F. Friggens for pew in S. Aisle	2	5	0
John Batten for pew in N. Aisle	3	14	6
Henry Vingoe for his pew		5	0

Whether the ordinary villagers had pews before this time is not clear; it would not be surprising if many had to stand.

At a vestry meeting in 1885 it was resolved 'that it is most desirable that an effort be made to restore Madron Church to a condition worthy of the sacred purpose for which it was built.' It was further decided at a later meeting 'that in carrying out the proposed work it might be necessary to interfere with or remove certain vaults, gravestones, monuments and mural tablets… but we undertake to use the greatest care and decency… and to refix the same as near as conveniently might be to their former positions and to re-inter any human remains which it might be necessary to disturb.'

All the old pews were swept away, and open and uniform pews put in their place. Heating apparatus and eventually lighting were installed, and the chancel was re-floored, so by 1889 the church emerged looking much as it does today.

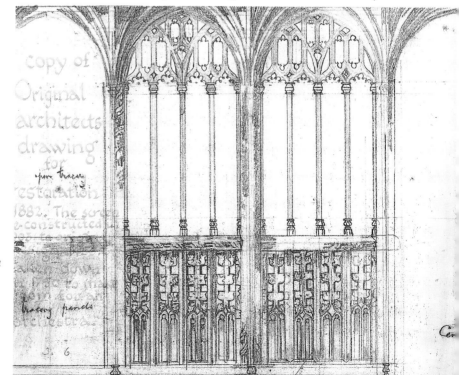

A copy of part of the original architect's drawing for the late Victorian reconstruction of Madron Church

Music in Madron Church

Although little is known of the state of music in Madron Church until the middle of the 18th century, it is likely that services reflected trends elsewhere in the country. For example, quite complex church music in Elizabethan times was an integral part of worship, while in the 17th century the Puritans were strictly opposed to all musical instruments in churches, so the services became an intoned duet between the parson and the clerk, with the choir joining in the metrical version of the psalms.

As only a few villagers could read, the clerk gave out the psalm line by line, then announced the tune. Amusing, if apochryphal, stories are told of misunderstandings, such as the clerk who, having announced the psalm tune, was troubled by the dim daylight, saying aloud, 'It is so dark I cannot see,' which was solemnly chanted by the choir. Exasperated, he shouted, 'Oh, ye poor fools, what fools ye be,' which was also duly intoned before the choir realised their mistake.

The earliest records of music at Madron begin in 1765, with entries in the churchwardens' accounts. The following selection throws some light on the subject. (In 1764 William Borlase became curate to his father Dr Borlase and continued as curate, then vicar, till 1812, a period of 48 years.) Annotations in square brackets are those of Canon Jennings.

1765   Two Psalm-tune books 2s. 4d.
Mr Jas. Mitchell 38 new books £3 2s. 6d. [there was a goodly number in the choir and efforts were made to make them efficient]

1765   to expenses with the Madron singers at Leggo's 6s. 0d.
to Ebbert Sampson, 11lbs of candles for the singers 6s. 10½d. [the usual charge was 1s. at Christmas, the heavy extra must have been for practices]

1767   Wm. Wilson's expenses with Penzance singers £1 7s.

1779   Expenses on Paul singers 15s.

1780   Expenses on Ludgvan singers 15s.

1781   John Courtney for books for the singers £3 10s. 6d.
Expenses on the singers, getting them a dinner and drinks by order of the parishioners £2 10s. 0d.
to John Courtney for teaching the singers, £20 for one year.

The next book is missing and accounts resume in 1807 by which time the singers are supplemented by an orchestra, violins, cello, double bass and tuning fork. They still had visits from neighbouring choirs.

1807   Expenses on St. Just singers, £4 7s. 0d.

1809   Pair of clarinets and reeds and music, £5 14s. 0d. [the parish clerk adds that this expense was disallowed at the vestry. Were clarinets too noisy for some?]

1810   New strings for 'cello, 9s. 5d.

         Singers on the day of the Jubilee [George III] 10s. 6d.

1812   Choir at Christmas, £1 1s. 0d.

1813   Book of music, 9s.

         strings for bass violin, 4s. 6d.

         Singers from Gulval £1 5s. 0d.

1815   New Strings £1 9s. 6d.

         Illuminating church tower after Waterloo, singers and ringers £5 5s. 0d.

1817   New strings for 'cello, 10s. 9d.

1818   Singers at Christmas, 18s.

1822   Expenses for Paul singers, 18s. clarinet reeds for three years, 6s.

1826   New clarinet £1 8s. 0d.

1827   New German flute and 'cello strings, £3 14s. 0d.

The records are then missing until the next reference to music in 1845. We know that in 1840 a barrel organ was introduced, probably as part of the widespread campaign to raise standards of church music. With pipe organs expensive and players hard to come by, a barrel organ required no skill save that of turning the handle at a constant speed. Being small and mobile, it could also be wheeled around, perhaps even across the road to the Five Bells pub for music of a rather different kind! This was not uncommon practice at the time. An entry from 1845 reads 'New barrel for the organ £1.1s. 0d.' What happened to the orchestra, and why, we shall probably never know; there is no further mention of music or singers.

A new pipe organ replaced the barrel organ on 30 October1859. In 1869 an organist was paid £10 per annum and the choir members received £10 10s. 0d.

A tune book compiled and written in 1800 by Tobias Reed, parish clerk of Madron, contains the familiar Christmas tune 'O come all ye faithful'. This tune is supposed to have been brought from Portugal, and 1800 is an early date for its use in England, so it would appear (or so Canon Jennings believed) that Madron must have been one of the first places where it was sung in England.

The Church choir around 1946. The crucifer was D Davies

Church choir

During the late 19th and early 20th centuries, the thriving church choir of men and boys were rewarded for their weekly efforts by an annual treat. They took the train to Truro and steamer to Falmouth where they had dinner and tea, returning in the evening at 10pm. In 1900 they went as far as Torquay and the next year to Plymouth to see the Hoe, Guildhall and Docks, and to take the steamer to Cawsand. Sometimes the destinations were nearer to home, to Newquay to walk to Crantock Church or to play in or watch a cricket match.

Organists changed over the years, but the choir remained strong. When in 1946 Mr E Weymouth, organist and choirmaster, returned from the Forces, he found himself running the largest choir ever known in Madron. At this time there were 11 trebles, 5 sopranos, 3 altos, 6 tenors, and 8 basses, and there were no vacancies. 81 clothing coupons were donated mostly in ones and twos to provide the lady members with appropriate caps and gowns.

Sadly choir numbers today have declined, but thanks to Robert Croft and his wife Helen there are still sufficient numbers to lead the morning church services.

Ding Dong mine

With tin and copper mines abounding to north, east and west and even one to the south on Penzance sea front, it is a little strange that Madron has only one mine within its parish boundary and that one high on the moors adjoining Gulval. This, however, is the famous Ding Dong, a giant among mines.

Ding Dong almost certainly has a very long history, even if most of it is either lost altogether or shrouded in obscurity. In the chronicles of 13th century King Henry III, a Cornish mine called 'Din Dods' was referred to as employing 100 men. This was probably our mine.

There is an intriguing theory – no more, no less – based on the name Din Dods as meaning 'the head of the lode' (Din being a high spot – as in Castle-an-Dinas or 'the castle on the high ground'). There could well have been an outcrop of tin ore on the hills above the Mên-an-Tol which the miners exploited, whereas before they had just searched the valley bottoms for 'streamed tin'. So, theoretically the art of mining, of digging for tin, may actually have had its Cornish beginnings in Madron.

Our scant knowledge of the mine is mainly from the 19th century when it was then properly called Wheal Malkin and of the 200-300 people employed one third were boys under 15. From 1818 it was owned by John Hosking, a one time resident of Landithy Farmhouse, Madron Churchtown, who is credited with having built the present Lanyon Farmhouse. The mule house still stands, where the animals were kept for their work of transporting the tin to the smelting works.

We know that in 1822 the mine was 100 fathoms deep and in 1872, 125 fathoms below adit, and that it went down to 148 fathoms before it closed in 1878 – not because it had run out of tin, but because of overseas competition which sent the price of tin plunging. In its heyday extraction of tin at Wheal Malkin yielded an average yearly value of £5000.

There is probably plenty of tin still there, for there were 22 tin lodes over the 500 acre sett and the underground tunnellings are very extensive, something like 9 miles of workings altogether and a great number of shafts. Few other relics of Ding Dong remain, however. Perhaps the chief one is the bell which is kept in the church. Another interesting item is a miner's candle and holder once worn by a Madron boy who at the age of nine was employed underground. There is also a (privately owned) tin match case – with the original matches – that was used by a miner underground at Ding Dong and which came up with him on the closing shift in 1878. He was a Madron man by the name of Friggens.

This bell, kept inside the Church, belonged to the famous Ding Dong mine, which according to Cornish folklore was so old that it had been 'worked before the Flood'

So the mine closed, having for very many years provided employment for miners both from Madron and further afield, and brought prosperity for the smelters, bankers and merchants. In 1965 a whole row of dilapidated cottages, which at one time were entirely occupied by miners, was demolished in Madron Churchtown.

Dame schools

Prior to the Education Act of 1878, which brought in the beginnings of universal state education, there were two small 'child minding' establishments in the village.

One, managed by an old lady, was above the King William IV, up a narrow stone stairway outside the classroom. It is said the children used to fight for the privilege of fetching ½d. of snuff from Mrs Richard's shop for the teacher. They were taught to recite long passages from the Bible, but one parishioner whose grandmother went to classes stated that her granny could only make noughts and crosses and was quite unable to read or write. It was probably more a place to keep children safe while their mothers were busy than anything else.

The other 'school' was in Fore Street in a cottage belonging to Nancy Jeffery

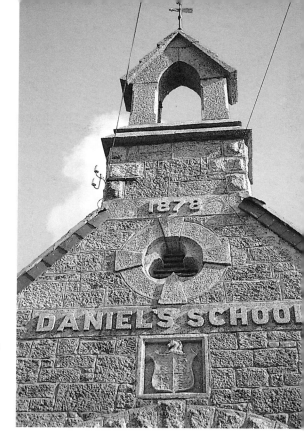

Madron's village school was established by George Daniel, long before education was generally available to ordinary children.

It is recorded of George that, having provided the school and a house for the master to live in, he donated a further sum for boots and bread for needy scholars, and a big saffron bun on Christmas Day! In addition each child was presented with a bible when they left and took up a trade or went into service, a tradition still kept up today for school leavers

who had a disabled sister Jane. The girls played, did crochet and knitting, while the boys had to read, and fetch water from the pump and snuff from the shop. Attendance during the summer holidays cost 6d. a week.

Village school

Madron is justly proud of its village school. Early in the 18th century, at a time when the education of children in Britain was seen as neither necessary nor desirable, Madron had the great good fortune to be presented with a fine, purpose-built establishment and a generous endowment for it to be run on sound financial lines. A plaque near the west end of the church's north aisle records this highly unusual bequest:

> 1710, A Free School in Madron Churchtown with certain lands bequeathed by George Daniel Esq., for supporting a Schoolmaster to instruct Poor children from Madron, Penzance and Morvah.

Just how enlightened Daniel's gift was can be judged from the fact that it took another 160 years before the government decided it ought to do something about national education. So George Daniel is held in high esteem in the village.

On 23 March 2001 Bishop Bill Ind unveiled a plaque to mark George Daniel's outstanding contribution to the community, and the children created a special ceramic picture also dedicated to their benefactor

His restored tomb, which also commemorates his father, Alexander, with a quaint verse – 'Belgia me birth, Britain a breeding gave, Cornwall a wife, ten children and a grave' – is in the churchyard overlooking his foundation.

George Daniel would be amazed to see the changes that have taken place in education in recent years and no doubt delighted that it is still his money which maintains the school building in such excellent order, complete with a computer suite and a pre-school class. Though the school has now taken the name of St Maddern, the trustees and staff have ensured George Daniel will continue to be remembered.

GARDENING CLASS. MADRON. 1920. 6.

Above: Gardening class in 1920

Below: The class of 1930-31

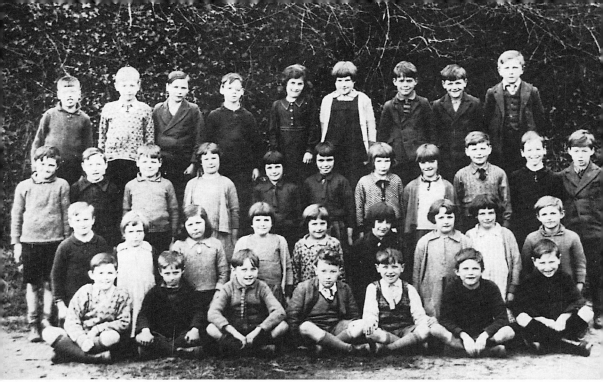

Above: The class of 1936-37

Below: Miss Simmond's class of 1959-60

Above: Mrs Cooper's class, 1961-62

Below: Mr Monk's class, 1961-62

Above: The school as it stands today

Below: Mr Monk and his family. When he retired as headmaster about 1970, he went to Zennor as Vicar

Sunday schools

In the past many children benefited from Sunday schools in Madron, Morvah and Heamoor. At Madron there was an annual prize giving, usually in February after the diocesan schools inspectors had visited and examined the boys and girls separately. Madron was reported to be 'one of the best schools in the diocese'.

In 1896 the prizes were awarded for regularity of attendance, but a warning was issued that 'in future years no child would receive a prize unless they obtained a certain proportion of marks and above all marks for good behaviour. Boys and parents please note.'

Technological progress shows itself when in 1913 the children had a cinematograph show in Landithy Hall (in use by 1911) at their annual prizegiving, whereas in 1902 the same event was followed by a gramophone and lantern slide show illustrating the voyage of the Prince and Princess of Wales in the *Ophir*.

Each July the three Sunday schools looked forward to their yearly treat at Trengwainton. It was free to scholars and teachers, but parents and friends had to pay – 6d. and 9d. respectively in 1898, for instance. At the 1906 treat there were 260 scholars from Madron and Morvah, and altogether 384 children, parents and friends.

The event followed a regular pattern until the 1914–18 war when the extravagance was curtailed in line with wartime difficulties, and it became restricted to scholars and teachers only.

A service was held at the church at 2 pm and after this the children processed behind a band to the Union House to 'cheer the inmates'. They then proceeded to Trengwainton for tea, sports and games, returning to the church at about 9 pm. They finished by singing 'God Save the King' before dispersing homewards.

In 1914, just before wartime austerity began to bite and prizes became donations to the County of Cornwall Motor Ambulance Fund, we have a very full report of the proceedings at Trengwainton:

> A cricket eleven from Madron Boys (who have practice facilities) beat Heamoor boys (who have no such facilities). A comfortable tea was provided for the 20th time by Mr Chirgwin [a family grocer and provision merchant with shops in Penzance, Heamoor, Newlyn and St Ives].

There were races and competitions for which prizes were awarded. Boys received writing cases, post card albums, chocolates, dominoes, a cricket outfit,

With the Reverend W Rowett in charge, a nativity play performed around 1973

purse, spade, racket, bucket, tie box, cricket ball, draughts and board, toy pistol, drawing slate, model yacht and mouth organ.

The girls had a glass box, trinket box, post card album, inkpot, work box, doll, skipping rope, dressed doll, doll's piano, chocolates, push cart, spade and bucket, paint box, writing case, purse, tea-set, ball. No wonder they all enjoyed it so much!

The popularity of Madron Sunday school can be deduced from attendance figures. In 1915 there were 136 under 12s and 178 older ones. By 1918 there were too many children aged 3-15 to be properly taught, so they were divided into six classes under six teachers on Sunday afternoons. The school continued steadily until 1946 when numbers showed a decline. Attractive coloured stamps were distributed as an encouragement to attend, and these were well received. Numbers rose again to 80 children who regularly went to matins.

By 1951 the Sunday school was giving prizes to all the Infants for 'merit, long and regular attendance' and was insistent they were not a bribe to attract children. Gradually, however, attendance declined once again, and by 1981 the Sunday school ceased.

Other children's groups

Various children's groups were started; some foundered, some thrived. In 1897 there was a Children's Union of the Good Shepherd – 1d. a month, open to all boys and girls, but this is hardly mentioned again in the records.

More successful was the Girls' Friendly Society in operation in 1907. The Misses Borlase of Castle Horneck were its patrons. Annual festivals were held, providing a band, tea at 9d. or 6d., and entrance 3d., with cakes, dairy products and ornamental items for sale. The society, numbering 27 in Madron, was part of the Penzance and Land's End branch which had 99 members in total. The last recorded festival was in 1917. A Band of Hope ran for a while, from 1912-14, giving concerts and organising outings to Porthleven.

During March 1918 a Children's Union, open to girls aged 7 and upwards, was formed to meet in the evenings. This was associated with the Church of England Waifs and Strays Society. Their aim was to provide money and clothing for the upkeep of 30 disabled children supported by the society, and also to knit socks and scarves for the troops. Initial membership was 21, rising to 30 the next month. Requests were made for wool and other materials which the younger children made into dolls' clothes. A year and a half later their diligence was acknowledged in a letter from the Matron of St Nicholas, Pyrford, Surrey, Church of England Home for Waifs and Strays, thanking them for 25 articles of clothing they had sent.

Madron Young Women's Club was formed in April 1918 and provided reading and recreation three evenings a week in the council rooms for girls over 16 years of age.

In addition to these attempts to enliven the weekends and evenings for young people, it was customary in agricultural communities for schools to make their holidays flexible to coincide with important events in the farming year. Boys and girls who were considered old enough were released to help at harvest times and during potato drawing seasons. But in November 1919 the education authorities declared a 'Universal August holiday for all day school boys and girls'.

Whilst this may not have affected cereal harvesting, there must have been quite a few unhappy parents and local industries who would previously have benefited from school pupils' availability. The older children themselves would also have missed out on money to spend on clothes and boots.

Boys' Brigade

Towards the end of the 19th century a branch of the Church Lads' Brigade was already flourishing at Heamoor, and in October 1897 Captain Maddern extended this to Madron. The village lads enjoyed exciting times under his direction. During their annual outing the following June, transported by Hutchens' Jersey Car, they dismounted and marched into Marazion, arousing considerable interest. Their ultimate destination was Pengersick Castle, but first they played cricket on Praa Sands, went in the sea or pottered on the beach. At Pengersick Castle they then had manoeuvres and sham fighting, having been divided into two sections led by Captain Maddern and Lieutenant Rodda, drill instructor and Company Lieutenant. The survivors had tea before returning at 7.30 pm on one of the finest bank holidays for some years.

The group went from strength to strength. By October 1909 a public meeting for all parents and boys aged 12-17 years led to the formation of the 1st Madron with Heamoor Company Boys' Brigade. Over 70 boys joined besides officers. They had 25 rifles in hand, but needed 45 non-firing rifles at a cost of £8 12s. 0d., uniforms and boots at £14 8s. 6d. and band equipment at £14 2s. 10d. At the next Feast service the north aisle was filled by the members who marched behind their band to arrive ten minutes before the service. Afterwards they lined up on the green where Mrs T R Bolitho presented their cards of membership.

Many of these boys saw action during World War I.

Girl guides and brownies

Girl guiding started in Madron in 1912, just two years after Baden-Powell and his sister Agnes founded the movement in 1910. Little is known of its early history except that Canon Jennings' daughter began the group which remained a stable unit for many years.

The guides were actively involved in village life and entertainment, attending Mount View, for example, to give a concert and tableau when Mrs T R Bolitho offered tea to the inmates.

We also know that Miss Joan Berryman was leader up to 1947 and that in the same year Mrs Wooldridge took over as captain, with Miss T Nicholls as lieutenant, and remained so until 1965. Miss Nicholls, now Mrs Winchester, then continued until 1971 when Mrs Caroline Summers became guider. By this time, however, the group was down to five members and it folded.

The group never went on camps or ventured far from the village, but they did attend a uniformed youth organization day at Culdrose where a trophy was

Guides and brownies at Trengwainton, around 1936

awarded for smartness and marching, after parades and inspections, which Madron proudly won in the 1950s.

They paraded on Feast Sundays and Poppy Day. Their banner was presented in 1948 in memory of Viola Elizabeth Low; it is now in the church.

Most guides started out as brownies who used to meet on Friday evenings at the guide and brownie headquarters above the stables in the grounds of the vicarage (now the Old Vicarage).

The Queen Mother visited Trengwainton for lunch one day in the mid 1950s and the brownies were thrilled to be asked to be the guard of honour, stationed before the front entrance. Mrs E Bolitho was the district commissioner.

It is sad to have to report that the Madron units have now ceased to exist because of a lack of leaders.

Cub scouts

In 1929 Miss Burstow and Miss Thomas, sister to King's Scout Gordon Thomas, ran the new cub group and continued with it until 1947. The group still flourishes today, attracting girls as well as boys between the ages of six and ten from Madron to Heamoor. There are beavers for 6-8 year olds and cub scouts for 8-10 year olds.

Scouts and cub scouts at Trengwainton, around 1936

Madron scout troop

In 1911 Major Venning began the scouting movement in Madron Parish. They first met in February of that year in a barn at The Reens Farm, Heamoor, before moving to Landithy Hall by kind permission of the Bolitho family where they continued to meet weekly until 1920.

Then they obtained new headquarters in a loft over the coal yard near 1, Poltair Terrace, Heamoor, but in 1928 Lieutenant Colonel E Bolitho offered them a plot of land at Hea Corner as a site for a more permanent headquarters. It was built by voluntary labour, Mr Fred T Berryman of Madron acting as clerk of works. Foundations were commenced in August – concrete blocks were made on site, each one attracting a donation from Lt Col Bolitho who laid the foundation stone the following July. The scouts assembled here until July 1941 when a German bomb destroyed the building. Fortunately it was empty at the time, so there were no casualties, and the original log book was saved.

The present headquarters were built as a replacement behind the British Legion Hall at Heamoor. In June 1969 Madron Scouts amalgamated with Penzance and are now known as Penzance, Madron Scouts.

In February 1986 the group celebrated 75 years of scouting in Madron Parish with a thanksgiving service in Madron Church. All scouts and cubs of former years were invited, and many who attended made arrangements to meet up again the following August at the international jamboree which they had last attended together in Cornwall in 1936. Among those present at the service were Mr Thorburn White, then in his 90th year, and Mr Gordon Thomas and Mr Jack Reynolds, both in their 80s; all three had been founder members. Also present were 'King's Scouts' – holders of scouting's highest award at that time.

To commemorate those 75 years of scouting, Eric Curnow, a Queen's Scout and former Madron scout, working in Baden Powell House in London, designed a badge for the occasion. A replica was carved in wood by Dennis Friggens on a piece of oak found in church from previous renovations. This was presented at the service to Reverend Roger Gilbert (another old scout) by Dr Bill Tellam, a patrol leader of the 1930s. It now hangs in the Lady Chapel. Commemorative mugs bearing the design were presented to all scouts and cubs.

Today Penzance, Madron Scouts go into the new millennium with enthusiasm undiminished.

Poor relief

In 1601, a Poor Relief Act was passed by Parliament. It was an early step on the road to finding a national and even-handed way of dealing with extreme poverty which for centuries had devolved to the Church. (During the medieval period, for example, the earliest hospitals, alms houses and free schools built through charitable acts to meet health care, housing and education needs were all inspired by the Church – although it was a very sporadic process, and benefits were bestowed rather haphazardly.)

The 1601 Act required each parish to be responsible for its own poor and the costs of the necessary aid to be paid for by a parish tax. All this was administered by the churchwardens and an appointed overseer, so the Church kept its close connection with village charity until a new Act in 1834 transferred those powers to Poor Law Commissioners.

The provision of poor houses was the usual solution for homelessness and destitution under the 1601 Act, and Madron parish had them at Hea, Penzance, Alverton and Trereife as well as in Churchtown. Of two poor houses in Fore St, one (No. 4) has the date 1812 over the door. All the details of their expenses and administration are carefully recorded in a set of Poor Law books from 1757 to 1841.

The cost of Poor Law Relief was kept to a strict minimum, most often to deter too many and too frequent callers on the service. Those accommodated in the poor house were bedded on straw. Furze was provided for fuel. Salt, soap and candles were also provided. Food included pilchards, barley, potatoes, carrots, turnips, cabbage, oatmeal and beef. There is no mention of tea, coffee or cocoa which were then expensive luxuries for the wealthy. Clothing was supplied but 'inmates' had to bear the letters 'MP' in red on their sleeves. Children, of whom there were five in Madron poorhouse in 1765, were given a modicum of schooling – thanks to George Daniel.

Some entries do bear witness to kindness on the part of the overseers – breaks in the clouds of meanness and the practice of bare existence. One such is the marriage of Ann Colenso, pauper of Madron, to John Thomas of Ludgvan. The expenses were paid by the parish and included:

Portion for the bride [dowry]	£5 0. 0.
Special Licence	£2 8. 0.
Ringers	4s. 0.
2 days expenses to arrange wedding	£1 6.10.

This represented a considerable chunk of the Poor Law income for the year.

A blacker side is shown in the treatment of those suffering from mental illness, as in the case of unfortunate 'J.T.' The following are just some of the items of expenditure for him in 1805:

To Shilton Keate, pair of handcuffs for J.T.	1s. 8d.
To Richard Victor for watching J.T. 2 nights.	3s. 0d.
To John Richards, boring a hole to receive J.T.'s chain.	10d.
Leeches to bleed J.T.	1s. 6d.
To getting a large stone and chaining J.T. thereto in state of mental derangement.	2s. 3d.
A bed cord for him	1s. 0d.
Canvas jacket for J.T.	12s. 3d.
For J.T. the people who watched with him 2 nights, his wretched condition requiring much attention.	7s.11½d.

And to end this horrific catalogue:

Funeral charges of said J.T.: coffin, 17s. 0d., shroud 4s. 0d., minister 2s. 6d., grave 2s. 6d., stripping 2s. 6d., certificate 6d.

To the people who carried the corpse	3s. 2½d.

According to Canon Jennings in 1936, 'The churchwardens and overseers appear to have been more generous in their treatment of the poor than any Public Assistance Committee would be today':

for two bottles of anti-scorbutic [scurvy] pills	£1 11s. 6d.

for two bottles of Dr Green's drops   11s. 0d.

Mr Davey for one gallon of wine to mix with bark for J.E.   12s. 0d.

J.E. did not appear to improve and shortly afterwards a more pleasant remedy was tried:

To forty-six pints of porter on doctor's orders for J.E.   11s. 6d.

There is even in the accounts an occasional glimpse of humour as in this little verse about a certain Mr Care:

1809 March 3. Set of castors for Care
                           To be fixed to his chair,
                           To wheel him about
                           To enjoy the fresh air.   Castors 1s. 4d. Fixing 8d.

Such lightness can surely have come only from a humane spirit.

Poor Law Relief was financed, as mentioned, by the parish. This was done by means of a tax on property. So householders' dwellings and land were valued and an annual rate of so much in the pound was levied. This varied with circumstances, the highest recorded rate in Madron being 7s. 4d. in the pound in 1820 when the total expenditure was £869 4s. 1½d., whereas in 1773 it had been only £101. Between the two dates there had been a steady increase. The following table shows the Rate List for Madron in 1826.

Madron's Poor Rate, Ladyday 1826

Tenements, Church Town	Names	Annual Value		
Tregodjack	Jas Glasson	18	0	0
Hse & garden	Revd Wm Tremenheere	4	0	0
2 fields under Tin field	Mrs E. Scobell	4	10	0
Moor & Croft	ditto		10	0
Ho & Garden	Wm Leggo	2	0	0
Ho's	Martin Hosken	3	10	0
Ho's	Frank Batten	3	0	0
Ho & meadow	Wm Friggens	1	0	0
Land	Mr Adams	6	10	0
Hos & meadow	Mr Batten Esq.	6	0	0
3 Ho's	Wm Rodda	3	0	0
Ho	Mr Rowe	2	10	0
Ho	Mr Richards	1	10	0
Ho & Shop	Wm Friggens	3	0	0
Ho	Rd Robarts		10	0

Pub Ho	Wm Mawer	3	10	0
Ho	Sarah James		10	0
Ho	Alice Trudgen	1	0	0
3 Ho's & Smithy	Tho. Wallis	2	10	0
Ho	Jane Leggo	1	10	0
Ho	Fras Dale	1	0	10
Ho	Mr Bosence		10	0
Ho	Mary Richards		10	0
Ho	Mr Rowe	1	0	0
Land	ditto	6	0	0
+ Trebean	ditto	4	15	0
Ho	Jos. Jeffery	1	0	0
Ho	Rd. Boase	1	10	0
Ho	Thos Hal		10	0
Meadow	Frank Batten		5	0
Pub Ho	Eliza Matthews	5	0	0
2 Cotts	Jas. Jenkin	1	0	0
Ho	Wm. Richards	1	10	0
Meadow	Wm. Mawer	1	0	0
Ho	Tobias Read	2	0	0
Smithy	Mr Jenkin	1	0	0
Vicarage	Jas. Bennetts		10	0

There were, however, one or two other sources of income which the church-wardens and overseers resorted to or dreamed up from time to time. It was their duty to arrange apprenticeships for young people growing up in poorhouses, and it was the principal landowners of the parish who were supposed to take the majority of these apprentices on. But occasionally, when there had been an unusually heavy demand on the Poor Law income, some of the landowners were brought before the magistrates on the grounds that they had failed to take on apprentices. Each was fined £10, which conveniently paid the outstanding bills and balanced the account. This, it would seem, must have come from a tacit agreement among the gentlemen themselves, probably to avoid setting a precedent of supplementary rate demands.

The following are a few entries from the Register of Apprentices in Madron and a list of the overseers of the poor in Madron from 1743 to 1773.

Extract of Apprentices' Indentures from 'A register of all the Useful Papers in the Parish Chest, 1805'

Apprentice's names	date of indenture	to whom bound	on what estate or holding
Sampson, the son of John Nickless	24th June 1732	Wm Arundell Esq	of Trengwainton
Thomas Dale	27th Der 1760	Thomas Hoskin	Then one of the overseers of the poor.
Anna Tackaboard	1 Sept 1775	Mr Saml Woodis	in respect of his estates in Madron
Jacqueth Roach	12th Augt 1780	Francis Trethowan	Landithy Lower
Mary Richards	5 Feby 1808	Ann Vinicombe	Madron Church Town
Jo's Jeffery	5 Sep. 1817	Wm. Nickles	on Landithy
Margt Lugg	1 June 1821	Frc Johns	Landithy lower
Thos Rowe	5 Oct. 1821	Wm Nicholas	Landithy higher
Mc Trewheela	1 Mar. 1822	Mr Jenkin	Madron Ch. Town
Wm Tonkin	3 Mar. 1829	Matt. Nicholas	Landithy

List of all such persons as serv'd Overseers of the poor from the year 1743

1743	Edward Chirgwin, Thomas Harry
1744	William Argol, John Thomas
1745	William Freethy
	James Sampson
1746	Henry Eva, Richard Hall
1747	Thomas Glason, Jeremiah Jelbard
1748	Wm. John Lanyon, Ralph Coren
1749	John Rodda, William Robyns
1750	John Jenkins, James Dale
1751	William Gingle, James Cervis
1752	Thomas Carvosoe, Martin Hosken
1753	George Love, Thomas Murrish
1754	Henry Eva, Richard Hitchens
1755	Tho Jenkin of Tregavara, Richard Rawlings
1756	William James, Jacob Coren
1757	Thomas Harvey, William Leggo
1758	Arthur Boase, Ralph Rodda
1759	Benedict Harry, Richard Chetmeal
1760	Thomas Hosking, James Dale
1761	William Freethy, Stephen Glasson
1762	Peter Kneebone, John Keskeys
1763	Franicis [sic] Philips, Ezekial Dunn
1764	David Edwards, Richard Hall

1765	Thomas Kemp, Abraham Chirgwin
1766	Thomas Bolitho, Willm Rodda
1767	Mr. John Lanyon, Benedict Harvey
1768	John Friggens, John Morgan
1769	John Vinnicombe, Richard Dale Jnr.
1770	William Leggo, Richard Hall
1771	John Hosking, Philip Argall
1772	William Trethy, William Thomas
1773	Mr. Tho. Baynard, Wm. Nicholls

Besides relieving the destitute, the parish had a hand in helping other needy souls, mostly widows. One lucrative method was via burials in linen. It had long been the law that all shrouds should be made of flannel, to encourage the wool trade. If anyone chose not to be so buried, preferring linen instead, they had to pay a fine to the poor of the parish through the churchwardens. In spite of the fine, however, linen became very fashionable – if one can ascribe fashion to such objects. There were, for example, 32 burials in linen at Madron between 1744 and 1814, so the poor benefited greatly to the tune of £3 10s. 0d. a time.

Another source of charity to the poor were the fines imposed by the vicar for petty crimes such as drunkenness and poaching. Thus we have:

1744	Thomas Pidwell, for shooting and hunting with spaniels, 10s.
1745	Thomas Maddern, for being drunk, 5s.
1750	Received of John Carvosse, 5s. on order of Dr Borlase for defaming the character of Elizabeth Weeks.
	Received of John and Mary Warren of Sancreed for Sabbath-breaking, 2s.
1800	¹/₂ of Richard Rowe's fine for keeping a greyhound, £2. 10s. 0d.
	¹/₂ of James Glason's fine for keeping a lurcher, £2. 10s. 0d.

To these distributions to the poor were added the church collection at the quarterly communion service (which were the only collections taken in church at that time). So we can see that although there was widespread and chronic poverty in the countryside, there were also various ways to counter it by both collective and individual means. For example:

| 1832 | Dinner at the poorhouse to commemorate the coronation of King William IV, £1. 1s. 2¹/₂d. |

The tablet in the church records the gift of £80 from Captain Thomas Hosking for providing a dinner to the poor in the poorhouse every year on February 10, the date of Captain Hosking's birthday.

Distribution of sacrament money to the poor 19 May 1772

Whitsuntide Sacrament rec'd	£1. 0s. 1½d.
Distributed to:	
Jane Dale	2s
Mary Rodda	2s
Jane Hall	2s
Margt Davy	2s
Mary Foard	2s
Zenobia Carter	2s
?? Bennatto	2s
Margt Hosken	2s
Eliz Rodda	2s
Mary Nickles	2s
John Sampson Sexton	2s

No sacrament at Madron Michaelmas 1772, as the Mayor of Penzance took it at St Buryan.

The workhouse

As a result of a review of Poor Law Relief in 1834 a new Act abolished the poor houses system, ended at a stroke the Church's participation in official relief and substituted for it a system of poor law 'Unions', each of which was required to set up a 'well regulated workhouse'.

The following account (edited) of Madron Workhouse was written by Mr LM Richards, 'Belmont', Madron, in 1976:

> Built in 1838 at a cost of £4650 to house 400 people, the building catered for the whole of the West Penwith peninsula and was administered by the Penzance Board of Guardians. [Mr Ambrose Taylor of 'Clayhill' was assistant overseer at the 'Union', collecting rates from 1898-1927. At one time he owned all the houses from the Union down to the blacksmith's shop, including the Primitive Methodist Chapel.]
>
> The Union later became known as the Poor Law Institution and later still as the Public Assistance Institution. The rear isolation block was converted in the early 1970s into four flats for use as temporary accommodation for homeless families. (This part of the complex now houses the Madron Meat Company.) The central block, a four-storeyed granite building with cellars (now demolished), formed the main accommodation building, with married couples separated into the male and female

The Madron & Penzance Union Workhouse, an image of despair to generations of Madron's poor

wings. The warden's house and accommodation for the other staff formed the front of the complex, with the main entrance central to the building. A porter's lodge and stone pillared gates stood on the main road (Fore Street) entrance.

In the Madron Parish Magazine of 1895, Vicar Tremenheere records: 'At the annual Sunday School Treat, after a short service the schools set off under their banners, headed by the band. Their route lay first to the Union House to bring a gleam of sunshine to the poor people there.'

This is recorded as an annual occurrence in subsequent magazines.

The following extracts from a letter by Norah Scrase, Madron, 1975, published in *The Cornishman* paint a dismal picture of life in the workhouse:

56

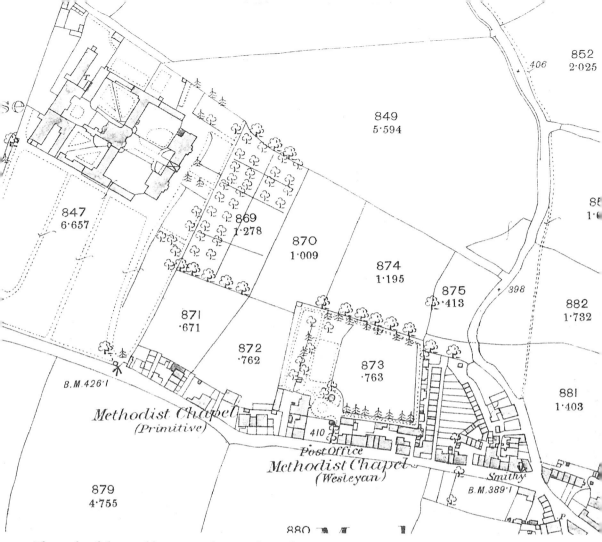

The scale of the workhouse can be seen from this map of 1878, where it dominates the top left of the map with its foursquare and mournful presence

Pausing to admire the former workhouse in Madron is not enough. Had Mr —— been inside when Mount View [so named in 1916] was a Poor Law Institution he would have changed his mind about it being well-designed. The windows are inserted so high up in the wall that even a giraffe would have had difficulty to look through them. How then must the unfortunate inmates have felt to be incarcerated in a cold room with concrete floors and dark green, distempered walls oozing moisture – with no chance of even seeing the serene view which gave the institution its name?

I speak from experience, as for many years I took a children's concert party there during the Christmas season. I cried then, as did many of the children, and I still feel saddened when I recall those dear inmates, husbands separated from wives, huddled together awaiting their keepers to get them off to bed as early as 4.30 pm only to spend long hours staring at each other, deprived of the panorama which spread itself at the foot of their badly designed last home…

I must make it quite clear that I am not an authority on the workings of the old Workhouse at Madron. Most of my knowledge has been gleaned from my own impressions.

My earliest recollections were firstly a 'pathetic collection of tramps' (not my words) making their way from Penzance to the workhouse, knocking on doors requesting some boiled water to be poured on tea leaves at the bottom of enamel cans, somewhat battered! If these people arrived at the workhouse without a permit they had to go back to Penzance police station to get one. When they were admitted to the workhouse they were bathed in strong carbolic water and their clothes were fumigated.

Secondly, I remember groups of boys and girls going to Madron School dressed in thick blue serge jumpers and skirts or trousers, black stockings and hob-nailed boots. They seemed to merge quite happily into the groups of local children at the school and were accepted as just more pupils.

Married couples were separated – those who were more able worked either in the laundry or were given general work to do. Bread and margarine seemed to have been the main food at most meals. Early to bed, between 4 and 5 seemed to be the order of the day. I can't comment on the staff. I'm sure they did their best in a very sad, unpleasant job. After all, they weren't in a position where their charges were getting better and looking forward to being re-habilitated at some future date. It always seemed to me to be such a hopeless set of circumstances. Of course there must have been quite a few attendants who were dedicated and behaved in a strictly Christian way. Scores of children and adults had been nursed for diphtheria, scarlet fever and all the other infectious diseases in the Isolation block which is now known as the 'Problems' – housing families who can't find accommodation elsewhere.

During the Second World War some boys from Devonport High School, Plymouth, were billeted at the workhouse, and their schooling took place in Penzance under their own headmaster. One man, known to the writer, who was there in his teens, tells how it was a vast, gloomy and grey place. He remembers an enormous bath tub filled with buckets of water into which as many as four or five boys were dunked once a week!

In 1946 the property was being used as a hospital and this continued until June 1951 when it finally closed. An article from *The West Briton* on 28 June, echoing many of Norah Scrase's comments, says all that is necessary to end the long, disturbing, yet not wholly dark story of Madron workhouse:

> The boys wore hob-nailed boots, and as most of them had been without boots or shoes in the nursery, their first schooldays were a torture, and a couple of boys helping a little friend to drag his feet along the road was a familiar sight. For breakfast they had a hunk of bread and porridge without milk; for lunch, broth, stew or pie; and for supper a variant on the lunch. The bread, say some of the old inmates, felt like wood.
>
> Almost any evening one would meet the casuals plodding up the steep hill for their bread and margarine and basin of cocoa and their night's rest on a straw bed. Before leaving, they were locked into a room and given a quantity of wood to saw. The room … was fitted with a barred window through which the pieces of wood had to be passed. If they were not cut sufficiently small, they could not be pushed through the bars, and until they were pushed through, the casuals were virtually prisoners.
>
> Every now and then, the dismal van – the 'Old Cober' as it was called – drove up to the big gateway with a crowd of crying children on board. The porter stepped out of his little box, the gates opened and closed, and another family was committed to the rough mercies of the 'Union'.
>
> Now the story of Mount View has ended for ever. That, perhaps, is the happiest and most important event to take place in Penzance Borough during Festival of Britain year; and certainly nothing could be more expressive of the Festival spirit with its emphasis on social achievement and its hope for the future.

The most famous resident of Madron workhouse was undoubtedly Alfred Wallis, the St Ives rag-and-bone man who took up painting late in life and became well known as a primitive artist. He died in the workhouse in 1942. This tombstone by Bernard Leach is in St Ives cemetery

Mr and Mrs Le Grice with Billy and Bobby at Trereife, 1960

Prominent families and houses

Although poverty was deep rooted and severe in and around Madron, there have always been families who by good fortune or good business acumen and enterprise rose above it.

In the 17th century, for example, the Maddern, Clies and Fleming families are described as 'gent.' in the parish registers, a sure sign of social standing. The first two of these could boast of having the first and second mayors of Penzance respectively (their memorials are in the church), whilst the Flemings were a very distinguished family who owned Landithy.

At the end of the 17th century John Borlase of Pendeen bought Castle Horneck and Roscadghill. In 1720 his son Walter was married, presented to the living of Madron by his father and installed in Castle Horneck. He was eventually succeeded at Madron and at Castle Horneck by his son William who died in 1812.

At Trereife, one of the oldest houses in the parish, were the longstanding Nicholls family. With the death in 1815 of William John Godolphin Nicholls, unmarried, aged 27, title to the estate reverted to his mother who had been widowed in 1792 and who in 1799 had married the Reverend Charles Valentine Le Grice, the curate of St Mary's Church, Penzance. The Le Grice family has continued to live at Trereife.

60

Rosehill, an elegant Regency house built in 1814, was the property of Richard Oxnam in the 19th century. Oxnam was active in parochial affairs

Lanyon used to be the property and residence of the Lanyon family. It comprised a substantial farmhouse and a chapel, of which nothing remains on the 471-acre estate. A report in 1965 by Mr Jewell, recorder for the Old Cornwall Society, refers to dated stones from possibly 1763, an ancient pound to accommodate straying beasts and a splendid mounting block with perhaps the top stone being the chapel altar. Opposite Lanyon farmhouse he was once shown by Mr C C James a 'smugglers' hole' or hiding hole (in a field which now only contains broken earthenware).

Trengwainton

By the 18th century several large houses, many of which still stand today, had already been built or rebuilt. The nearest at hand, Trengwainton, was owned by John Cowling until his death in 1666. A branch of the Arundell family then acquired it but later moved on to Kenegie in Gulval, changing their name to Harris in 1780.

An intriguing Harris tale reveals that 'on April 7th in that year, in consideration of the altar plate donated to Madron Church, all mines to be discovered or worked on his property were to be exempted from payment of the poor rate'. A well judged and timely donation no doubt!

Sir Edward Bolitho and his wife Agnes at Trengwainton. In May 1931 Sir Edward invited the public to the garden for the first time

Sir Rose Price was the next owner at Trengwainton. In his more leisured years after his wife died, he planted large numbers of trees (some of which still stand) – the forerunners of the windbreaks so important for today's tender species. He also constructed the unusual walled garden with slopes for growing early produce. However, the Slave Emancipation Act of 1834 more or less ruined him, and in 1866 Trengwainton was bought by Thomas Simon Bolitho, perhaps the most successful member of a prodigiously successful family. So began the long period of enthusiastic and dedicated involvement which has led to the garden's present status as one of Cornwall's and the country's best.

Thomas Robins Bolitho, son of T S, enlarged the house to its present size in 1897 and built the splendid carriage drive down to the lodge. T R was followed by his nephew Lieutenant Colonel Sir Edward Bolitho who really transformed the garden into something very special. He was ably assisted by the head gardener, Alfred Creek, who skilfully propagated so many wonderful rhododendrons and magnolias from seed brought back from plant hunting expeditions to the Far East. The stream beside the drive, today a lovely feature, was also opened up.

In May 1931 Sir Edward invited the public to the garden for the first time and for the rest of the decade successes were gained in prestigious Royal Horticulture Society Shows.

Above: The magnificent gardens at Trengwainton

Below: The unusual walled garden with slopes for growing early produce

After the war period, during which the trees and shrubs were neglected and as much ground as possible was given over to food production, the garden was brought back to its former glory. In 1961 Sir Edward was presented with the RHS Victoria Medal of Honour for horticulture. In the same year he made the garden, but not the house, over to the National Trust which arranged for it to be opened to the public.

Since then it has continued to be influenced and supported with knowledge and enthusiasm, first by Sir Edward's son Simon, then by his grandson Colonel E T Bolitho OBE.

'In house' memories

The big houses provided employment for many village people – girls as under-maids who lived in, women as housekeepers, men as gardeners, grooms, butlers and house servants. It was a hard life perhaps, but it was secure, with food and accommodation provided.

As several of the houses had farms attached, there were also leases available and some of the farmers became rich gentlemen. These in turn needed domestics to live in and plenty of labourers.

This aspect of local affluence continued in a gradually declining form until the outbreak of the Second World War ushered in a totally new era of rural life.

Many people can remember working at Trengwainton House in their younger days, some forty or fifty years ago. One such person who lived in is Louie Nicholls (née Friggens, born 1909). She tells of demanding but happy work as a kitchen maid. When she started, in 1929, there were: a cook, a scullery maid, a kitchen maid, three housemaids in a hierarchy of first, second and third, and a parlourmaid, all under the beady eye of a butler.

Louie used to get up at 6 am. There was a black range to clean with 'Zebo' and a kitchen floor to scrub before she cooked breakfast at 8 am for eight servants. She had time off on the first and third Sundays in the month from 10 am-1 pm, and on the second and fourth Sundays from 3 pm-10 pm. The girls were allowed, with the butler's permission, to go home for dances so long as they were in again by 11 pm – and he did check them in.

The housemaids and parlourmaid worked upstairs, the kitchen staff stayed below stairs. They all had a uniform to wear but the parlourmaid, who waited at table and also cleaned glass and silver in the big pantry, changed hers in the afternoons for a coloured dress and small white apron. The kitchen staff wore their uniforms all day. Louie's was home-made, a dress with grey and blue spots on a white ground and a big brace apron with an embroidered cap – which she removed when no one was looking! Nanceglos, down the road a little from Trengwainton, took care of the laundry and was also used as a schoolroom for Trengwainton children.

The family consisted of Colonel and Mrs Bolitho, son Simon and daughter Ann who spent plenty of time visiting the kitchen as a child. Nearly all meat and vegetables for meals came from their farms and gardens, so they were largely self-sufficient. In fact, the gardens provided much employment. Fruit and vegetables were ordered up the day before, being required when menus had been prepared by Lady Bolitho. Sometimes meat was brought from the town, but all had to be there after breakfast. The cook/housekeeper ordered groceries.

Louie went twice to Scotland for the grouse shooting, staying for a month or more, and remembers well the journey on the sleeper from Euston to Forfarshire, then to Tongue, and being chauffeur-driven to John O'Groats. Pheasant and grouse cleaning also left a lasting impression: 'They were hung until green as a leek with maggots crawling out!'

Chapel

Methodism in Madron has played a long and beneficial role in village life. The background to it, of course, lies in the great religious revival, particularly strong in Cornwall, brought about by John and Charles Wesley in the latter half of the 18th century.

Thirty-one tours of Cornwall were undertaken by John Wesley, including sixteen to the Penzance area. Why so much attention to Cornwall? Because at that time it was a large and important centre of industrial activity. There were thousands of uneducated miners and their families living lives which were impoverished in every sense, often existing in abject wretchedness where lawlessness and depravity reigned.

This was the scene which the established church was largely failing to grapple with and upon which the Wesleys, after initial suspicion and hostility, wrought their miracle of evangelising, instilling into hardened hearts a love of God and a determination for amendment of their moral life.

John Wesley preached time and time again – St Ives, Morvah, Tregavarah, Penzance, Gulval and 'on the downs at Hea' where he used as his pulpit the famous rock which is now incorporated into the chapel at Heamoor. The fervent atmosphere and deep involvement at those meetings are now difficult to imagine, but the effects led to the building at Madron, and all over Cornwall, of the simple yet dignified chapels that became the lively centres of religious and social life in the village.

According to F W Hoare in 'The Old Chapel' (Madron Old Cornwall Society Notes, 1951), there were two early methodist meeting houses in Madron Churchtown. The first Wesleyan chapel, the oldest in the circuit, was built in 1800, about 40 years before the erection of Wesley Rock in Heamoor. Further up Fore Street there was the meeting house of the Primitive Methodists which later was used as a store and was then converted into a house (now known as 'The Old Chapel'). One of its stalwarts was Warwick Cock who died during World War I when his son Thomas James Cock was serving with the army in India.

In 1901 much earnest consideration was given by the trustees of the old Madron chapel to a planned new chapel. By September the choice of architect had fallen on Mr Maddern and he was asked to submit plans for a building to hold 175 adults at 20 inches per sitting plus a schoolroom for about 100 children. John Samuel Tregenza of Mousehole won the building contract which stipulated that the work should be finished by November 1902 for a total cost of £1050 and that a penalty of £3 per week would be imposed for excess time.

The stone-laying ceremony took place on Friday 13 June 1902, but by the time the interior was finished and provided with a heating system, and Mr J H Vingoe had been appointed chapel keeper at £4 5s. 0d. per annum, a year had passed. So it was not until 30 June 1903 that the chapel was actually opened for its first service.

The old chapel, which was situated on the other side of the road from the new one, was pulled down and the site is now occupied by bungalows. The small Wesleyan chapel at Boswarthen (now converted into a house) was sold to boost funds.

Mr Bill Cock has in his possession mallets used at the stone-laying ceremony by his mother Agnes Leggo and his uncle Ernest Leggo. He also has the mallet used by Flossie Dunstan, while the one used by John Jenkin, superintendent of the Sunday school, is owned by Mrs Mary Friggens. Without doubt there are several others in the locality.

Chapel interior

The two tablets (with work by Charles Hoare) on either side of the pulpit, containing the Ten Commandments, were a gift from Mrs Watts. The large brass plaque is in memory of John Jenkin, while the clock was given in memory of William Charles Leggo, an original trustee.

 A second brass plaque is in memory of Minnie Matthews who was organist for 35 years, and an electric organ was given by the Cock family in memory of Thomas James and Agnes Mary Cock. The flower vase and stand in front of the pulpit were presented by the Madron Women's Institute in memory of Agnes

Psalm cxxii. .. .. Rev. T. H. BANKS, B.A.

Prayer .. .. Rev. W. H. MAY.

Hymn.

CHRIST is our corner-stone,
On Him alone we build;
With His true saints alone
The courts of heaven are filled!
On His great love Our hopes we place
Of present grace And joys above.

O! then with hymns of praise
These hallowed courts shall ring;
Our voices we will raise
The Three in One to sing;
And thus proclaim In joyful song,
Both loud and long, That glorious Name.

Here, gracious God, do Thou
For evermore draw nigh;
Accept each faithful vow,
And mark each suppliant sigh;
In copious shower On all who pray
Each holy day Thy blessings pour.

Here may we gain from heaven
The grace which we implore:
And may that grace, once given,
Be with us evermore;
Until that day, When all the blest
To endless rest Are called away.

First Stone	..	..	Mrs. W. J. BAZELEY.
Second Stone	..	..	„ F. HOLMAN.
Third Stone	..	..	Miss FLORRIE RICHARDS.
Fourth Stone	..	..	Mr. J. HOSKING.
Fifth Stone	..	..	Master T. O. ROBERTS.
Sixth Stone	..	..	Mr. JOHN NEWTON (For the Trustees).
Seventh Stone	..	..	„ W. BENNETTS.
Eighth Stone	..	..	„ THOMAS PENROSE.
Ninth Stone	..	..	„ ERNEST TRIGGS (For the Local Preachers).
Tenth Stone	..	..	„ JOHN JENKIN (For the Sunday School).

Part of the stone-laying ceremony for the new chapel, from the official programme

Young People's Hymn.

JUST as I am, Thine own to be,
Friend of the young who lovest me
To consecrate myself to Thee,
O Jesus Christ, I come!

In the glad morning of my day,
My life to give, my vows to pay,
With no reserve and no delay,
With all my heart, I come!

I would live ever in the light,
I would work ever for the right,
I would serve Thee with all my might,
Therefore, to Thee I come!

Just as I am, young, strong, and free,
To be the best that I can be
For truth, and righteousness, and Thee,
Lord of my life, I come!

Young People's Memorial Stones,

— LAID BY —

Master COLERIDGE CARMAN
Miss LILIAN MAY COX
   „   CHARLOTTE ANNIE DALE
Master HARRY DALE
Miss FLOSSIE DUNSTAN
   „   ANNIE HALL
   „   FLORRIE HAMILTON
   „   MABEL V. LABRUM
   „   GERTRUDE LAWRY
   „   AGNES LEGGO
Master ERNEST LEGGO
Miss POLLIE LEGGO

Miss CLARICE MATTHEWS
   „   LOUIE MICHELL
                (Kenegie, Gulval)
   „   MAY NICHOLLS
   „   JANIE PHILLIPS
   „   FANNY TRELOAR
Master GORDON UREN
   „   ARTHUR R. VINGOE
   „   ARCHIE WHITE
   „   GRAHAM WHITE
Miss SARAH MAUD WHITE
   „   WINIFRED WHITE
   „   IRENE MARY WILLIAMS

Address .. .. Rev. E. J. BRAILSFORD.

Offertory for New Chapel.

Doxology. + **Benediction.**

The stone-laying ceremony took place on Friday 13 June 1902

The interior of the Chapel

Mary Cock, and in the front of the chapel is a wrought iron flower stand given in memory of Mrs Phyllis Penberthy.

In the entrance lobby is a carved wooden book rack (whose ends depict the tools of the blacksmith's trade) which the Stevens family donated in memory of John Hosken Stevens. Most of the plentiful copies of books and bibles have been given in memory of chapel members who have passed on – James Penberthy, Eric Semmens, Betty Docking, Wilhelmina Maddern, Rose Goldstone and the Matthews family.

Reggie Green, who was a local preacher and member of the chapel, painted the two images of Christ which are in the Sunday school.

The radiator in the vestry was given in memory of George Goldstone (both chapel and schoolroom are heated by an oil-fired boiler using the original pipes of the old solid fuel boiler), and electric lighting was installed in memory of Mary Jane Dale.

Chapel services

Madron is a member of the Penzance Circuit. The superintendent Minister, currrently the Reverend John R Izzard BA, is based at Chapel Street, Penzance. Madron's section includes Richmond, High Street, Gulval and Wesley Rock.

The Methodist Chapel Anniversary Service, traditionally held in the open air at the Baptistry

Sectional events are organised such as an annual service at Gwennap Pit, an Ascension Day service at Chapel Carn Brae and study pilgrimages around the area featuring various chapels built by Billy Bray.

Madron also organises special services in its own church throughout the year, including the Chapel Anniversary (commemorated on the first Sunday in May when it is traditional to hold an open air service at Madron Baptistry), a Sankey Evening in May, a Maundy Thursday supper (held in the Sunday school), a Good Friday service, Harvest Festival, a Festival of Lessons and Carols and a Christingle service.

Chapel and Church work closely and happily together, particularly at Madron Feast when a combined service is held at the church in the morning and the chapel in the evening. The guest preacher is invited by the Anglicans one year and the Methodists the following year. Church and Chapel likewise share the service which is held after the Old Cornwall Society's annual 'Crying of the neck' ceremony.

The King William IV

This old pub has always been a lively centre of village social life on a par with church, chapel and WI. It is a much used and loved meeting place with a long tradition of fine singing, including visits from the Mousehole Male Voice Choir and a wealth of home grown talent from the Matthews and Friggens families, and from the likes of Albert and Eddy Strick and others.

At one time the singers were so keen that when the pub closed for the night, the harmonising went on at the blacksmith's shop across the road! On Feast Sunday the regulars, with many lubricated reinforcements, turned out into the road and began the season of Cornish Christmas carols in great style.

The pub interior has been much altered over the years. Early memories are of one long bar parallel to the road; long tables and forms for seating; a Bottle and Jug bar where the present entrance is; and a Snug at the far end.

Publicans have included Mr Birch, who gave up his teaching post at the Daniel School in about 1927 to run the pub; ex-army man Mr Carter, who died in the job and whose wife carried on for many years, ruling with an iron hand; ex-naval man Joe Denley, whose daughter married a builder who built Little Boskinning (on Trafalgar Sunday the sailors were welcomed by Joe to quench

The King William IV in the 1880s, when the landlord was John Mitchell

Above: The King William IV, approaching from Heamoor

Below: The King William IV in 1965

Mr and Mrs Southern, before they emigrated to Western Australia

their thirst after the service); and Mr Osborne, ex-army and also very patriotic – how and why a big drum came to roll out of the pub in flames on one particular Trafalgar Sunday was never adequately explained! The Southerns, too, ran a good pub where the old traditions flourished until they emigrated to Perth, Western Australia. There was also ex-police sergeant Kendal who, as was the fashion of the time, installed a juke box which sadly killed the fine old singing tradition stone dead.

Women's groups

We are fortunate enough to have preserved in our parish vestry chest bound copies of the Madron Parish with Morvah magazines dating from April 1895. From this rich source we can deduce something of life in Madron over a considerable period.

Many of the groups formed were led by the ladies of the parish, such as Mrs T Robins Bolitho of Trengwainton, the Misses Borlase of Castle Horneck, Miss Bolitho of Trewidden, Mesdames Trelawney, R Nicholls, C A Borlase, and J White.

In 1896, for example, Mrs Robins Bolitho started a Mothers' Meeting which met monthly. Seven years later it became the Mothers' Union. The ladies enjoyed an annual treat together, going to such places as Praa Sands by wagonette and on one occasion an outing by train to Falmouth. There they boarded the steamship *Victoria* at 2.30 pm bound for Truro for evensong. The cathedral was at this time newly built, and for many of the party it was their first visit. They ended the afternoon with tea at Clarke's Restaurant, returning in brakes to the railway station whence 'The Cornishman' brought them home.

Those whose lives were not too encumbered formed a Ladies Working Party in 1902. They presented 50 hassocks for the kneelers in the church on Easter Eve. As they had a balance left out of their budget, they set about improving the kneeling accommodation in the choir stalls too.

Later, in 1915 St Katherine's Guild was formed within the church. They had enrolment, rules and a guild prayer, and were responsible for the cleaning of the church, the brass and linen, and needlework for furnishing of altars, cassocks and surplices. This devoted and valuable work continued into living memory, and now there is a band of volunteers who undertake the cleaning of church and brass.

Madron Women's Institute

The Women's Institute (WI) has the proud distinction of being the first to be formed in Cornwall. It was begun before the end of the First World War, in 1918, by Mrs Robins Bolitho who became the first president.

In the WI's early days focus was on important issues of the time. There were talks on fruit bottling, laundry work, citizenship, housing, infant welfare, and there were literature readings and debates, including 'The effect of the Cinema on Modern Life'. But there was also relaxation and enjoyment in the form of organised outings and events.

Stella Triggs, a former president of the Women's Institute, who acted at the Minack Theatre

In 1919 members ventured out in brakes and wagonettes to Cape Cornwall, and to Carbis Bay the next year. They played badminton and whist, had lantern lectures, competitions for wild flowers and held many social evenings when members' children could attend for 1d. and non-members for 3d. Dancing was very popular and a monthly dancing class took place.

1928-38 saw the period of great agricultural depression which caused financial hardship all over Cornwall, so the emphasis turned very much to thrift. Making thrift rugs from old stockings and rags, even a husband's shirt tails, became popular. But even in those hard times, or because of them, a tennis club (season ticket 4/-) was formed, picnics were organised with tea and cake (extra cakes 1d. but 'bring your own cup') and there were treasure hunts, skipping competitions and much fun locally on Madron Carn and at Trengwainton.

Mr and Mrs J Reed, who started the May Revels

Annual May Day Revels were organised too.

Then the 1939-45 war broke out. Members turned their talents to finding ways of coping with shortages in food supplies. They learned ways of using soya flour as a nutritive supplement to the national flour available, how to make non-meat dishes, to dry herbs, nettles, foxgloves, mint, etc, and they enthusiastically picked berries for jam making.

Money was raised for soldiers', sailors' and airmen's charities. When Truro hospital was bombed, funds were raised to help replace lost equipment. Parcels were put together for prisoners-of-war. However, these deeds still left the WI feeling remote from the real war effort, so many members joined the Women's Voluntary Service to play a more active part.

In all the difficulties imposed by shortages, Madron folk pulled together and village life was more active and enthusiastic than it had been before or has been since. By 1946 the WI's membership had risen to 140 (at the 1920 AGM 65 members were present).

Above: A post-war May Queen, June Semmens, at Landithy Hall before the Revels

Below: Children and the May Queen, Rosalie Hollow, at Landithy Hall, about 1938

Joan Berryman leads a pre-war May Day procession at Trebean

Even by 1935 a drama group had been formed which co-produced with the Madron Players. They performed *Trial by Jury*, then *Jim Eny's New Dog*, followed by *Old World Cornish Star* in 1946 and *The Great Day* in 1949. The group went from strength to strength and, although no longer together, in their day became well known far beyond the parish for their drama.

Madron WI children's fancy dress party, around 1960

Above: Madron Players and WI Drama Group in The Great Day, *1949…*

Below: …and in a skit on Penzance Town Council

Above: Madron Players produced The Bride and the Batchelor *in December 1969*

Below: The Young Players give a party for the over 60s

Trereife, home of Mr and Mrs Le Grice, was always welcoming to WI members and friends – many strawberry teas were consumed here!

1953 was Queen Elizabeth's coronation year. The WI presented any member who had a baby with an engraved coronation spoon. Instead of May Revels they held a special Coronation Revel and the Queen wore a golden crown. All the children wore white with a red, white and blue sash.

In 1968 the WI celebrated their golden jubilee. Many cups were won in county competitions and at the spring show in Penzance and elsewhere. 'Tree Planting Year' provided an opportunity for action and members planted 240 trees. By 1978 Madron WI was 60 years old with a 'kaleidoscope of achievement' behind it. Great celebrations took place. Seven other institutes, all formed 60 years ago (but after Madron's), were invited to send their presidents to a grand dinner at Landithy Hall. St Just joined Madron at the Queen's Hotel for a celebration: the Madron institute had been formed in the morning, and St Just's in the afternoon, so it was a close run thing!

As part of the diamond jubilee celebrations, Trereife, the home of Mr and Mrs Le Grice, was opened for a tea party. Five hundred members and friends attended, and a pageant, written by Mrs Le Grice, showing people who had lived at Trereife since the 16th century, took place on the lawn.

The WI is still thriving and, like Mrs V Nicholls and Mrs L Nicholls, two veterans who have been members for most of that time, still enjoying its activities which have expanded to include surf boarding, gliding, and archery, showing that the WI is indeed not just 'Jam and Jerusalem' – although it never was!

Other groups

Early snapshots

Given the chance, Madron villagers have always been keen to help themselves in difficult times. In December 1879 ninety-seven members formed the Madron Provident Society. They saved regularly, 2d. a week throughout the year in a clothing and coal club. When the twelve months were completed they received a due allocation of coal, their savings for clothing and a bonus which varied annually according to the increasing number of members. The club had a long life and was obviously very beneficial.

The village was also generous as far as it could be during the 1914-18 war. Mrs Andrew Stevens knitted 136 pairs of socks and 17 mufflers. The Band of Hope sent knitted scarves to the front. An egg collection service was started in 1915. Madron wives and farmers delivered eggs to Landithy Hall in August for convalescent and wounded soldiers. 47 dozen over three weeks were added to others from elsewhere in Cornwall and this continued for the rest of the war.

Choral society

A choral society was started at the end of 1901 by Mr Nunn who was succeeded in 1905 by Mr Sellers. Accompanied by a string band, they gave concerts in the council school at Heamoor. Tickets were 2s. 6d., 1s. 0d. or 6d.

In 1910 they took part in a special concert on Easter Tuesday at Landithy Hall to mark its opening (this fine hall was built at the expense of Thomas Robins Bolitho in memory of his father Thomas S Bolitho). And in 1912 Mr HV White conducted his first practice meeting which was open to all parishioners.

Since then, Madron has continued to provide musical entertainment. A recent remark at St Mary's Church, Penzance, sums it up quite simply: 'Madron is known for its music'.

Cottage Garden Society

Madron Cottage Garden Society was a very popular group and held annual exhibitions at Trengwainton, the first in July 1908. In 1911 there were 400 entries, an independent band was in attendance, and morris dancing was performed by the children in the afternoon – the adults had their dancing in the evening.

Today Madron has several allotments for keen gardeners, although they are less used than previously, and the West Cornwall Garden Club has taken over from the old Cottage Garden Society.

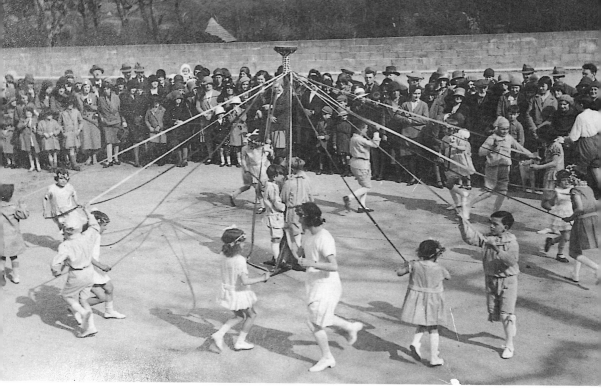

Maypole dancing in the school playground, about 1930

Royal occasions

Kings and queens come and go, incidentally providing opportunities for everyone to celebrate and have a good time.

A full record exists of the village's celebration of 'the 60th Anniversary of the Accession of our Gracious Queen Victoria' in June 1897:

At 1.15 pm all Parishioners are requested to meet as far as possible at the 3 centres detailed below and, headed by their bands, to advance 4 deep at Trengwainton Lodge, the children leading the procession.

1.   All south of the St. Just Road and the Trengwainton Stream are requested to meet at Trereife or join the procession en route.

2.   Draw a line from Lesingey to Bone and all the parish south east of that is requested to meet at Heamoor School.

3.   The rest of the Parish is requested to meet by the Daniel School at Churchtown.

At the Lodge the children will advance first up the drive and the adults follow. A tree will be planted, the National Anthem sung and the children will then have tea at three o'clock, followed by the adults at the time stated on the tickets they receive and to which it is necessary to adhere.

There will be swings for the children and a programme of sports.

The WI's pageant celebrating the Festival of Britain, 1951

The sports included maypole dancing, ornamental skipping and egg and spoon races for girls, and sack, three-legged and donkey races for boys; there was also a tug of war contest among teams from Heamoor, Trereife District, Churchtown, Bossullow and the rest of the parish, as well as a cricket match between Madron and Goldsithney. Unfortunately the event was stopped by heavy rain at 5 pm.

When Queen Victoria passed away at Osborne House in February 1901 in the 64th year of her reign, a memorial service was held at Madron Church, timed to coincide with her cortège travelling from London to Windsor.

Now Edward VII came to the throne, and by chance before he was officially crowned he visited Madron. He does not appear to have done much more than pass through however!

Nevertheless, the village planned to spend a large sum of money on entertainments to celebrate his planned coronation. The event was delayed when the horrified nation received news on 23 June that the king was lying seriously ill and needed an operation to save his life. To everyone's relief he was out of danger by the end of June, so a large bonfire was lit on Tregavarah Down as a mark of thanksgiving, but no further mention is made in the records of a village coronation celebration.

In 1907, during Edward's reign, Empire Day was instituted. On 24 May all the parish children were invited to Trengwainton. 900 attended with neighbours and friends. Mr T R Bolitho explained the purpose of Empire Day, hymns and the national anthem were sung, and then they had tea, sports and competitions.

King Edward passed away in May 1910. The Countess of St Germans organised an address of condolence from the women of Cornwall, together with a funeral wreath to be laid beside the coffin. The sum of £6 7s. 6d. was sent from Madron's 401 subscribers.

In April 1911 the country prepared for the coronation of George V and Queen Mary. Miss Bolitho of Trewidden and Miss Warren of the Lodge, Trengwainton, proposed to collect a subscription from 1d. to £1 to commemorate this event by presenting a gift to the queen. Only those bearing the name Mary, May, Maria, Marie, Marian or Marion were permitted to subscribe. The coronation took place on Thursday 22 June, which was made a public holiday. Churches throughout the land held a service at 11 am to coincide with the coronation.

King George V had a long reign. After his death in 1936 he was succeeded by George VI on the abdication of Edward VIII. During these years of the Great Depression, followed by the Second World War, there were few celebrations and photography was not readily available to the private individual to record such as were held. But in 1951 the country as a whole blossomed into the spirit of the Festival of Britain. Madron took part in several ways, the villagers all uniting to enjoy themselves after the years of shortages and privations.

The children performed their *Pageant of Empire* on Penzance Promenade, along with maypole and country dancing, and the WI presented a pageant on the church steps. After the Old Cornwall Society had tidied up the Baptistry, the annual service was again held there in July when Delia Hodge was baptized. By the end of Festival of Britain year a 'family spirit' was very noticeable about the parish – great efforts had been made to spruce Madron up.

King George VI died in 1952 and with typical Madron spirit 600 people packed the church at the time of his funeral. A call to worship was made on Trinity Sunday, two days before Queen Elizabeth's coronation on 2 June 1952 when a specially authorised service was to be held. On the Monday at 7.30 pm all the youth groups took part in a youth vigil.

On Coronation Day itself the ringers rang a grand peal at 9.30 am and Mr J Reed planted a tree in the churchyard at 10.15 before the service, which lasted from 11 am-1.45 pm. So many attended that people stood outside to listen while it was relayed to them. A television set was put in the Daniel School 'with no guarantee of good reception', but 'some parts of it were all right'. In the after-noon the children received coronation mugs at the George V Memorial Field where sports were played and a tea was put on.

As a grand finale in the evening a vast bonfire was lit on the Carn, accompanied by a sing-song, an open air dance and a £50 firework display.

The rejoicings lasted all week. Perhaps the most astonishing spectacle was a comic cricket match between men and women (with cross dressing), during which Muriel Semmens bowled her father, Madron's champion batsman, from the pavilion end, neatly removing middle stump! Most of the village were there to watch and a pasty supper ended the evening's event.

After the coronation, few wartime restrictions remained. The church was floodlit, the village decorated with bunting and flags, and Reverend Hocking showed the film *The Meaning of the Coronation* to local groups.

Madron Feast

Madron Feast began, it is thought, after the building of the church tower and south arcade, and consecration of the chancel and high altar, on 13 July 1336. It may have been kept on this date until the church was completed by the building of the north aisle about 1500, and then altered on re-dedication to the new date.

Madron now enjoys a celebration of the Feast of St Maddern from the first Sunday in Advent. In 1909 it was held on two days. On Sunday, celebration followed much the present pattern – a morning service attended by all, or most, but on Feast Monday there was a concert in the Daniel School, the profits going to the choir fund. In 1902, entrance was one shilling.

Names mentioned as performers during several years of concerts are: Miss Chads (recitation), Miss M Chads (violin), Miss Grant (mandolin), Miss Leigh Bennett and Miss M Tregonning, Mr and Mrs Lionel Birch, Mr Chappell, Mr W Paul and Mr Bill Adams, Mrs Brindley and Miss Beaulands (accompanists).

In the late 19th century the Western Hunt became an integral part of the celebrations with a Meeting on Feast Monday morning. And goodness knows what was happening in 1911 for the vicar to issue a reminder to his parishioners that 'the Feast is a Church Festival and ought to be kept soberly and religiously'.

The feast was held annually on the same lines until 1917 when there was no feast tea. Instead, the Sunday service was followed by an afternoon organ recital. The next day entertainment was put on at the school, and the concert takings were sent to the Sailors' Fund.

'By Feast Sunday 1918, the Armistice was three weeks old, so there was great rejoicing. It proved to be the best for years,' according to the parish magazine.

The Western Hunt meets on the morning of Feast Day, around 1957

The Archdeacon of Cornwall attended the church service, muffled bells were rung; half the service was held in church, the other half on the memorial site. Nearly 1000 attended from all neighbouring parts and the keys to the memorial gardens were handed to the chairman of the Urban District Council to show that henceforward the gift would be in the Council's care.

The memorial, which had previously been draped in the church's flag, was unveiled by Mr T R Bolitho who had given the cross and land to the village (a typically generous gesture from a man whose family constantly supported the village in many ways, from providing venues for events to building Landithy Hall). A well attended evensong took place.

'The Monday Concert Party was decimated by influenza, demobilisation and leave but did its best on a night of fog and penetrating rain... Dancing followed.'

Agnes Mary Cock's memories of the Feast in the earlier part of the 20th century, recounted to her family and handed down, tell of stannings (stalls) in the pub square, limpets in vinegar and gas torch lighting. Feast became extended to a week's festivities by 1946. The bell ringers heralded the Sunday by ringing a great peal at 7.30am. The Western Hunt met next day on the Green, as was the custom. In the week that followed there were bazaars, socials and other forms

The church clock, which
exhorts us to
'Watch and pray,
Time hastes away,'
was a typically generous gift
from the Bolitho family in 1999

of home-made entertainments. Children had a school holiday. Mr A Southern, landlord of the King William IV, provided the hunt Stirrup Cup in 1965, a custom carried on by today's landlord, Peter Ede.

With so much involvement by so many people, long live Madron Feast as a uniting force in the community!

Reverend William Tremenheere

The Reverend William Tremenheere was vicar of the Parish from 1895 for nearly twenty years until in October 1914 he announced his retirement. He and his wife were prominent in the guidance and welfare of a large parish which extended much further than at present. He was assisted by a curate. He kept good records in the parish magazines and wrote of national events as they happened, marking the death of prominent men such as Gladstone in June 1898 with a ring of muffled bells and the Dead March played at matins and evensong.

During 1898 the parish also suffered the largest number of deaths for ten years from influenza. It continued at least until March the following year. The Boer war (1899-1902) saw men called away for military service and the Lych Gate was dedicated in November 1904 to commemorate it.

When in 1905 a new hymnal was introduced to replace the 1860 *Hymns Ancient and Modern*, the new edition was received with mixed feelings but it was apparently retained for use.

The Reverend Tremenheere was not averse to making comments on the political situation either. The Liberal government's Education Bill, which proposed removing religious instruction from all schools and Church control from Church schools, put the Daniel School's position in jeopardy. The Act forbade schoolchildren going to church in a group on Ascension Day, as they had done for years following the founder's express direction in his will. But parents were reminded by the vicar that they could bring their children individually!

The *Titanic* sank in April 1912 and there was a national coal strike; all was reported upon in the parish magazine. Great relief was felt in the parish when on 5 January 1914 the last payment on the vicarage was made. Built by the predecessor of Reverend Tremenheere with a 30-year loan from Queen Anne's Bounty, it had cost the Reverend John Tonkin MA £1566, a heavy burden for him. For some years the Reverend Tonkin had paid a third of the yearly charge, and the lady patrons the rest. After his death the ladies paid the whole. So we can deduce that the Old Vicarage was built in 1884.

The outbreak of the 1914-18 war was forecast in August's magazine of that year. Austro-Hungarian hostilities against Serbia occurred. Price rises in food,

The Old Vicarage, probably built in 1884

In 1915, the Men's Fellowship cleared and cleaned up the churchyard, and brought the Norman font basin back into the church, from the churchyard where it had been discarded. The newer font stands on the base of the Norman one. Now parents had a choice of font for their babies' baptisms

troubles in Ireland, British troops' involvement in Belgium and Northern France where the Germans were attacking – all upset life.

The Reverend Tremenheere left the parish on 6 November 1914 and moved to Bath. He was presented with an illuminated address, a purse containing a cheque for £214 4s. 2d. and an album bearing the names of subscribers.

The Reverend Colville, who succeeded him in December 1914, had once been curate of Calstock parish, a large living in south-east Cornwall; his mother was Cornish. He came to Madron from South Beddington where he was curate for ten years, then vicar, and was considered 'go ahead'. He had had a new church built with a congregation of 6000.

He did not flatter the parish with his first impressions of Madron. In his third magazine he wrote of Churchtown and District: 'The great illusion locally is perhaps the great value to its incumbent of the living of Madron... The time has come to speak out... Madron with its three churches, its workhouse duties and its scattered population... offers no prospects either of ease or wealth... it cannot offer its Vicar anything more than unlimited work and a very limited income, both to be enjoyed in healthy and pleasant surroundings.'

In 1914, the Church of England's Men's Society formed its own branch in Madron (it already existed in Heamoor at St Thomas'). Also a church council came into being with twenty-two members – the two church wardens and clergy being *ex officio*, and representatives from St Thomas' and the parish church. By 1920 Madron Parish Church Council was set up.

Baptistry services

In the Reverend Colville's time it was decided to re-instate a service at the Baptistry, to be held on Midsummer's day – the Feast of St John the Baptist. The Bishop of Truro sanctioned administration of baptism if desired.

The first service was held on 4 July 1915. With church bells ringing and St George's flag flying, the procession left the Green at 2.30 pm. There were crucifers, servers, choristers, three clergymen, school children, teachers, visitors and congregation members. The mossy stone at the Baptistry was covered in 'fair linen' and lit candles, and from there holy sacrament was then taken at the Holy Well. The service was over by 4 pm and a last benediction was given at 4.30 pm in the church. Reports appeared in the *Church Times* and *The Guardian*.

The service became an annual event and baptisms took place there regularly. A parishioner remembers that her father was once taken to the Well for triple immersion, then laid in blankets on the altar while God's blessing was sought in

Choristers processing to the Baptistry in 1946

prayer. Some of the recorded baptisms are:

> 4 July 1915   Marjorie and Ivy – children of Frederick William and Evelyn Burch; Daisy Rosalind, daughter of Albert and Bessie Semmens.
>
> 26 June 1916   Ida May, daughter of William Thomas and Jane Elizabeth McCoy.
>
> 23 June 1918   Edward Paul, son of Richard Seymour and Pauline Paynter.
>
> 22 June 1919   Norman Tippet, son of Adolphus and Hilda Stinton.
>
> 20 June 1920   In the presence of the Bishops of Truro and Barking: William Chesney, son of William and Mary Kelynack; William Charles Allenby, son of John Nicholas and Emily Gendall; Gladys Irene, daughter of Thomas Charles and Lily James.

The bell ringers

Those who live within earshot are well accustomed to the sound of the church bells which ring out on practice night on Monday, on Sunday to announce a service and sometimes on a Saturday to herald a wedding. The solemn sound of 'muffled' bells indicates the passing of a loved one of the parish or occasionally of a figure of national importance.

At the beginning of the 18th century Madron, like most Cornish parishes, had three bells. Then came an upsurge of interest in ringing and in 1761 Madron decided to sell its three old bells and invest in a new peal of five. These were ordered from Bayley of Bridgwater. There then followed a long period of expense and frustration. The third bell had to go back to be re-cast but continued to cause trouble; it was re-cast at Helston, and again, at Loughborough. Two others of the peal were unsatisfactory until re-cast at Hayle Foundry in 1823.

Finally all was well for many years, but in 1898 it was decided that they needed renovation. This happily coincided with Queen Victoria's diamond jubilee, so to commemorate the occasion a sixth bell, a treble, was added. The bells which rang out over the village for decades after were:

1. Given in 1898. Inscription: 'God save our Queen and Church. William Borlase Tremenheere, vicar.' Weight 4cwt 0qr 5lb.
2. Re-cast Hayle 1823. Inscription: 'Rev. W. Tremenheere (vicar), Jas. Glasson (churchwarden).' Weight 4cwt 3qr 3lb.
3. Cast 1761. Inscription: 'Walter Borlase (vicar), Thos. Jenkins (churchwarden).' Weight 9cwt 2qr 8lb.
4. Re-cast Loughborough 1842. Inscription: 'Rev. Michael Nowell Peters (vicar), P. Kempe (churchwarden).' Weight 4cwt 2qr 27lb.

The White family (from left, Arnold, Kathleen, Thorburn, Dorothy and Graham) donated the seventh bell, inscribed 'In memory of John Kemp White, 1867-1947, Choirmaster and organist. His children's gift.' Weight 3cwt 2qr 19lb.

The bell ringers in 1948

5.   Re-cast Hayle 1823. Inscription as number 2. Weight 6cwt 3qr15lb.
6.   Cast 1761. Inscription as number 3. Diameter 38 inches. Weight 4cwt 2qr 23lb.

   Like all other Madron groups the ringers enjoyed annual outings within and beyond the county boundary. A notable happening among these was in 1898 when the Madron cricketers, playing at Troon, were supported by the ringers so enthusiastically that they succeeded in defeating these formidable opponents. Many outings involved visits to other churches to ring peals.

   Since 1911, festivals have taken place in parishes such as Madron, attended by members of the Truro Diocesan Guild of Ringers from Penwith and other deaneries in the Duchy; therefore it might be true to say that the bell ringers are the oldest established group still functioning in the parish today.

   In 1946 there were 18 bellringers in Madron: Mr G W Thomas was captain and the committee consisted of chairman, the vicar, vice-captain Mr A White, instructor Mr T W Tayson, towerman Mr J Nicholls, honorary secretary and representative Mr J W Reed. The other ringers were Messrs T R and Rob. Wooldridge, C and W Semmens, N and W Friggens, S J Robinson, T Tucker, J Johns, J Maddern, Mrs W A White and Mrs W F White.

   In June 1950, a motor cycle scramble, with a dance afterwards, raised £950 to enable the bells to be re-hung. Two bells were added at Madron, the seventh by the White family (see page 93) and the eighth bears the incription 'The Gift of the Truro Diocesan Guild of Ringers. In memory of John Symons MRCS'. Weight 4cwt 0qr 0lb. All eight were dedicated on 3 March 1951.

In the early 1980s, a glass screen was installed to prevent draughts blowing from the ringing chamber. Being mindful of the financial restraints upon the parish, in the mid 1980s Madron ringers decided to take matters into their own hands to raise revenue. New bell ropes were required, the cost of which was nearly £1000 and, in consequence, the Madron Ringers Thrifty Club was born and is still in existence today. This fund-raising scheme became an annual tradition not only in the parish but throughout many counties of England!

Hitherto, access to the ringing chamber was gained only by using a ladder which was hung vertically against a wall and which led to a trapdoor in the floor of the belfry. Over the years many complaints were made about this entrance to the chamber and some visitors flatly refused to use the ladder, which meant they were unable to ring in the parish.

Much time and effort were spent in the investigation of an alternative access and eventually it was decided that the most effective method would be to install a wooden staircase and to insert a door into the screen. The ringers raised the total cost of around £3000 and it was with some delight that on Trafalgar Sunday in 1998 the staircase was first used and was dedicated.

On 1 January 2000, Madron ringers rang the bells at 12.00 noon, accompanied by fellow campanologists throughout the country who rang in their respective towers in a concerted effort to welcome the millennium.

Madron Old Cornwall Society

On Wednesday 1 October 1924 in Landithy Hall the Reverend Canon Jennings introduced Mr Morton Nance to a large gathering of Madron folk who had come to hear him talk about the desirability of forming an Old Cornwall Society in Madron. Mr Nance was already well known for his intimate knowledge of things Cornish which were being rapidly forgotten – dialect, history and stories of the area, how things used to be done in the farming world, local names of fields, games and amusements and rhymes of days gone by...

If a society were founded, it was explained, the speaker, in keeping with tradition, would be expected to sit in front of his audience and not on the platform, for it was not a Learned Society but a group of friends interested in Cornwall's ancient heritage. Rules would be minimal. A committee would be needed, consisting of Cornishmen and made up of a president, secretary (also to act as treasurer) and recorder (recorders log discoveries and keep details of vital historical importance on all aspects of Madron parish, such as field names, family names, farms and houses, flowers, birds, archaeological discoveries; in fact anything which adds to the historical record).

Left: The original Madron Old Cornwall Society banner. Right: The Old Cornwall Society's display at the 2000 Flower Festival in the church

Mr Le Grice proposed that a society be formed; Mr Cooper seconded. The motion was carried and the following were elected: president, Mr Le Grice; secretary and treasurer, Mrs Dickson; recorder, Mr Reed. Entrance was set at 1 shilling for adults and 6 d. for those under 18. And so it was that the still flourishing Madron Old Cornwall Society was born.

With 76 members in 1930, many talks covering a wide range of topics of local interest came from people within the group. There were lessons, too, in Cornish. A party was held each new year, with guise dancing, plays and songs performed by talented and willing folk. Old time dancing concluded such gatherings.

Summer excursions were taken during June, July and August to churches and houses. Since few people travelled far at this time, those who did gave welcome insights on returning from their outings to Stratford-on-Avon, the Isles of Scilly, Isle of Wight, London and the Lake District. These were especially entertaining when lantern slides were available.

During wartime, meetings were suspended. They resumed in October 1949 when Canon Hocking presided over a meeting to revive the Society which Morton Nance addressed, as he had done at the original formation 25 years earlier. Membership grew slowly at first, attaining 60 by 1955 (tea, hot pasties and saffron cake became the normal refreshment from 1952), then increased until during the '70s it reached upwards of 150 members. Today members continue to enjoy excellent meetings held in Landithy Hall.

Two important Old Cornwall Society events take place annually, both of ancient origin: the midsummer bonfire and 'crying the neck'.

The midsummer bonfire (21 June)

In origin the midsummer bonfire was a world-wide pagan fire festival to mark the year's longest day. Traditionally, in Penzance bonfires were lit and blazing tar barrels and fiery torches were run through the streets. This exciting spectacle, to which crowds thronged from miles around, was eventually banned because of the fire risk.

Safer, if somewhat less thrilling, was the chain of hilltop bonfires organised by Old Cornwall Societies in 1929 throughout the Duchy, and annually from then on.

Madron's first bonfire was in 1954, on Trengwainton Carn, a popular and nearby high spot with spectacular views. The next year it moved to Bull's View, near Ding Dong Corner, where it is still held today. The event starts off with the singing of an old Cornish song, and a prayer in Cornish and in English. Then the bonfire is lit and into it the 'Lady of the Flowers' casts a bundle of herbs representing good and evil. The 'good' plants are St John's wort, rue, sage, saffron, foxgloves 'to calm troubled hearts', clover (for industry and unity), wild orchis (for beauty), vervain (the holy herb reputed to have grown at Calvary), green barley and wheat herbs, and an oak sprig for goodness and strength. The 'evil' plants are tormentil, the burning of which 'bane to the good husbandman' speeds the plough, brambles, docks, thistles, wormwood (for sweat and toil and bitterness of life) and Mayweed (for uselessness). These are all tied by coloured ribbons, each colour symbolising a different virtue: saffron for justice; red for sacrifice; white for purity; blue for truth; and green for hope. There are also amber and black ribbons, the Duchy colours.

The midsummer bonfire

Crying the neck

The following report in *The Cornishman* of 16 September 1967 by Mrs Mollie Bartlett gives a vivid, comprehensive and 'proper Cornish' account of this ancient ceremony which that year was enjoyed by some 200 people.

'Ansome Time Cryin' Th' Neck Up To Maddern.

I veel I mus' write to tell 'ee all 'bout th' 'ansome time we 'ad up to Maddern las' Zaterday afternune, when Penzance an' Maddern Old Cornwall folks performed th' old, old ceremny o' 'Cryin' th' Neck'.

My friend Jane was in long o' me th' week avore an' she catched zight o' th' notiss in th' *Cornishman.* ''Ere, seen this have'ee?' zes she. 'There's goin' to be a revival up to Maddern.'

'I knaw all 'bout it,' zes I.

'Is Billy Graham goin' be up there?' zes Jane.

'Never heard tell o' no Billy Graham up to Maddern,' zes I. 'Who's 'e?'

'I tho't everybody knowed 'bout Billy,' zes Jane lookin' at me as if I waz proper iggerant. ''E's a g'eat praicher wot been over 'ere vrom 'Merryka to convert folks.'

'Well, we don't want 'e up there,' zes I, 'we got praichers o' our own.'

Well, there was a purty g'eat crowd o' folks gathered up there in varmer White's cornd-vield to zee it done. Maister Orchard an' Maister Stinton, Maister Pool an' our vicar got together to start things off.

Th' crowd was chartterin' like a passel o' magpies but all o' a sudden they valled quiet when Maister Orchard started to ring th' g'eat bell from th' old Ding Dong Mine. T'was a glad zound too, diff'rent from the zad toll 'e made when th' miners cum up from the'r las' shift at Ding Dong in 1878. Maister Orchard showed us a water-proof metal match box which belonged to William Friggens and was used on th' very las' shift at th' mine. Matches still in un too – good's ever.

Then Maister Stinton took over an' tould us all wot was goin' to 'appen an' wot twaz all about like.

Then 'e asked th' folks where they'd come vrom an' as th' parties vrom St. Just an' all th' places round put up their 'ands, a g'eat clappin' o' 'ands zounded out. Th' folks 'ad cum vur miles roun' an' there was one or two vrom England too. One purty maid I spoke to was vrom Exeter University! An' there waz two 'ansome chaps there, one vrom Culdrose an' one vrom Portland Bill – th' very Air an' zay rescue chaps wot vished they two skin divers out o' th' zay out Lizard way 'tother day!

Cutting the last sheaf   *'I 'ave 'un! I 'ave 'un!'*

When Maister Stinton asked if there was anybody there vrom vurrin parts one boy standin' right avore me shot up 'is 'and! I gived'n a poke an' asked where e'd cum vrom when th' clappin' died down, an e' looked me straight in the eye an' zed 'Heamoor'.

Then we 'ad a prayer, virst by our vicar an' then in th' proper old Cornish by Maister Orchard an' after that Maister Stinton tould us all 'bout th' old ceremony an' wot twaz all 'bout. Seems nobody d'know 'ow it started – but tiz more'n likely twaz zum zoart o' 'eathen caper when folks tho't there was a spirit in th' corn that 'ad to be 'peased to make sure th' 'arvest would never vail.

Likely enough they offered up a sacrifice, p'raps a animal o' zum zoart. Zackly as 'e zed they words a dog dashed past like th' wind, barkin' like mad. I b'leeve 'e tho't twaz time to clear off! In later years twaz a matter o' pride which varmer should vinish virst an' 'cry the neck'.

Then Maister White throwed off 'is jacket an' rolled up 'is shirt sleeves an' laid 'old o' 'is s'ythe. I bet 'ed 'ad a good old go at'n wi' th' balker avore

99

Crying the neck ceremony, 1975

'e brot'n up there! An' then 'e putched to mow that las' 'race o' corn left standin'. Long, steady strokes 'e made, like th' men did in years gone by when th' las' piece was laid low. 'E bound it all up in sheaves makin' a 'bind' o' corn to hold each sheave together, an' twichin' a 'andful out o' each one to bind th' next.

Then 'e made a shock o' th' sheaves an' with th' strands twiched out o' th' las' sheave 'e made th' neck. 'I have'n! I have'n! I have'n!' 'e roared 'oldin th' neck up vur all to zee.

An' we all hollered back – 'Wot have'ee? Wot have'ee? Wot have'ee?'

'A neck! A neck! A neck!' roars Maister White an' we all cheered like mad.

Then Maister Pool done it all over agane in proper Old Cornish an' we all cheered agane. Then we zinged another hymn an' after that we went down to th' Church an' 'ad a lovely little service. Maister Monk spoke to us an' Missus White read th' piece vrom th' Bible.

After the service was over we trooped back to Landithy Hall for our tay an' 'ot pasties an' a piece o' Hevva Cake an' a chat wi' friends old an' new.

I shall never forget that afternune, twaz a thing to be proud of. In perticklar th' way th' zun come out and poured down in that one vield, while th' Mount an' th' Lizard an' all th' lozely plaaces round about could only be zeen vaint an' shadowy droo th' mist.

Like I zed. It zeemed to me like a blessin' and a bennydiction on wot we waz doin'. Then th' breeze that all o' a zudden zeemed to catch up th' zound o' th' g'eat bell an' waft it away back to Ding Dong – like 'e waz zendin' back a note o' hope to th' old mine. I veel sure everybody wot waz there las' Zaterday went away veelin' like I did, wi' a zence o' peace, an' pride too, in bringin' to life agane one o' th' dear old customs o' our grandfather's days an' I 'ope we shall keep it up too.

It all tooked me back over th' years to when I waz a little maid an' shared in all th' 'arvest customs. There's one more I'd like to zee revived; tha's th' 'Ay 'Arvest custom o' 'Makin' Sweet 'Ay'.

All th' chaps an' maidens'd come out to th' vields vur th' las' 'drinkin' gallons o' 'ome made zider an' 'spruce' an' zaffern buns an' pasties. An' then th' vun would start! Th' chaps'd chase th' maidens all over th' vield till they catched 'em an' kissed 'em good an' hearty droo a ring o' 'ay.

All these rings would be put in th' 'ay rick as twaz made to make an' to keep th' 'ay sweet!

I reckon if we could revive that old custom we'd stand a bra' gude chance o' bringin' th' young folks in an' stirrin' up their int'rest in th' old customs o' our young days.

After all, unless we can pass 'em on to th' youngsters, they'll die out an' be forgot an' we shall 'ave lost part o' that rich heritage of our past.

The Neck continues to be Cried in September each year, following the same pattern but without the summons of the Ding Dong bell. Penzance Silver Youth Band provides the musical accompaniment and the service is held in alternate years in the methodist chapel and the parish church where the Neck remains for the next twelve months.

Guise dancing

This is centuries old and was the main winter entertainment in the villages of West Penwith up to 60 years ago – Madron and St Just always used to vie with each other in guise dancing.

The word guise, pronounced 'geez', means disguise. All the participants wore masks or had their faces covered with a coloured cloth or sheet to look as hideous as possible. Each player contributed to the entertainment, singing, dancing or playing a musical instrument. In Madron the accompaniment was usually provided by a 'cardjul' or concertina. The last cardjul player was Bertie

Richards of Heamoor and the bones were last played by Tom Bottrell of Buryas Bridge, within the parish.

Over several generations the guardians of the custom were the family of Mr Billy Jenkin, blacksmith and village constable who died in 1912. He handed knowledge down to his son, also a blacksmith, who in turn handed it on to the great grandson, father of Mrs Sylvia Bowden, née Jenkin, Cornish bard and final custodian of the words and music. She helped revive the custom in 1996, having grown up from childhood with the annual guise dance.

She remembers how a group of friends used to meet and rehearse the mummers' play, 'St George and the dragon', at Mrs Pollard's Parc-an-Grouse farmhouse. Mrs Pollard played St George; her sister Jenna and Sylvia Bowden's mother played two old ladies sitting in a cottage where the dancers came. Other players were John Reed, headmaster, his wife Lily, who was described as very tiny but who played the Turkish knight, and Mr Bowden who played Beelzebub with a false nose. Phyllis Treborrow who worked for Mrs Pollard was Jacky Sweep and performed the broom dance which Sylvia could also do, being so familiar with the whole thing.

She also recalls how, one early January day in the 1930s, they had gone up the roads through Madron, over the fields to Boswarthen and Bulls View, past Lanyon Cromlech and down half a mile of lane to Bosullow to Lennox Green's barn. Hurricane lamps were hung up, a stage erected and chapel seats brought over for the audience. When they got on the stage the boards rattled plenty as extra accompaniment!

On other occasions they normally arrived in costume and unannounced at the houses, big or small, to entertain. St George's costume was by then 100 years old. (In 1996 Sylvia Bowden's niece still had Beelzebub's old hat.) After the play there was teasing, dancing and refreshment for the guise dancers before they left.

In 1995, 60 years after the last guise dance, a Penzance-born student at the University of Surrey, studying Dance in Society for her final year thesis, came to Madron to try to revive the ancient performance with the aid of local people whose memories of it were almost lost. With help from a committee backed by the Old Cornwall Society president Doug Davies, the Women's Institute and the Reverend Toogood, a group was formed which, after several false starts, eventually performed the guise dance once again before Christmas at Landithy Hall. Mrs Bowden gave invaluable advice and practical help with rehearsals, but unfortunately the event did not arouse as much enthusiasm as had been hoped and no further performances have taken place since. (Sadly, this was also the fate of the May Day Revels celebration once held in Madron.)

Guise dancers, 1936

The words and music still exist, so there is always the hope that perhaps one day someone with a theatrical leaning and an interest in Old Madron may once again try to resurrect this traditional entertainment. It does still exist in other parts of the country.

Madron in wartime

Remembered by John Cock

I was eleven years old when the war broke out in September 1939, and seventeen when it ended in 1945. I spent the whole of this time living in Madron, so probably can remember as much of those years as anyone still alive, apart from perhaps Mrs Mary Friggens.

In 1939 Madron was a small, rather poor village of about 340 people. Most men worked on the land, with a few quarrymen, market gardeners and carpenters. There was also the large workhouse or Poor Law Institution which up until 1939 had been fairly full. The outbreak of war soon meant full employment, so sections of the 'House' became empty for other uses.

The first impact on Madron was the calling up of the Militia in 1938. Men of 21 were drafted into the Forces, including one or two Madron men. As war

Civil Defence J6 Company, 1938-45. Back row: W Stevens, unknown, J Reed, A White; middle row: G Matthews, unknown, H Stevens, P Stevens; front row: unknown, unknown, W White, W Allen, T Beamish

became imminent, John Reed, Willie Allen and Wilfred White became air raid wardens. Everyone was issued with a gas mask in Landithy Hall. Infants and small children had special masks. We were told to carry these everywhere, first in cardboard boxes but later in more robust holders.

With war came the evacuation. Each parish had billeting officers. People had to take children according to their spare bedrooms. Many volunteered and took children cheerfully but some objected, and in one bad case two children spent many hours outside a house while the lady went off for the day, and when she returned she refused entry. Madron evacuees came from Millbank School, London. They were brought to Landithy Hall. Local people came to the hall and chose their children. This had the obvious effect of the pretty, well dressed children being quickly snapped up, leaving the more scruffy element for later arrivals. In the first six months of the war there was almost no bombing so many evacuees returned to London, although quite a few stayed and one or two settled in Cornwall. At first the evacuees had lessons in the Hall and part of Madron School, but as their numbers declined they became pupils of Madron School.

Madron was often visited by a Ministry of Information film van. This would show films on the Green about what to do in an emergency.

Willie Leah became a special constable to help PC Kersey, especially to check people's blackout. There was no street lighting and cars had headlight grilles. White lines were painted on roads to avoid accidents. Petrol was rationed, with most private cars getting very little, and many people laid their cars up for the duration. The bus service was severely cut, with seats put around the sides of the bus so that as many as 30 could stand. The last bus to Madron from Penzance, which had left the station at 10.30 pm, now left at 7.00 pm. It returned from Madron at 7.20 pm. After that you had to walk.

All food was rationed and the amounts were small: 2oz butter, 4oz margarine, 2oz lard, 4oz bacon, 8oz sugar, 2oz tea, one shilling and twopence worth of meat, 2 eggs. There was a points system for almost all other goods and for clothes and sweets. 'British restaurants' were opened in towns, where you could get a plain, wholesome meal. As Madron was too small for this, an allowance of meat was made available to make pasties which were sold for 7 d. each on Wednesdays. Our shop sold as many as 170 each week.

The war continued quietly until April 1940. More men were called up and the main action was at sea. The British Expeditionary Force with a number of Madron men went to France. A number of better off people came to live in and around Madron as they thought it was a safe area. The blacksmith's shop closed when Horace Jenkin went to work in Devonport dockyard.

The whole war changed in the months of April, May and June 1940. Madron men came home on leave after being evacuated from Dunkirk. I well remember Charlie Matthews spending the evening with us and telling of his dreadful experiences. A French fishing boat came into Penzance with badly wounded men after being machine gunned by German fighters. I remember a bus full of the less seriously wounded coming to the workhouse.

The first bombing raid on Penzance was in August 1940, when bombs fell on North Parade, Alma Terrace and the County School. My father, who was in Penzance getting the bacon ration for the shop, was knocked over by the blast and had to hunt for his bacon on his hands and knees. After that a number of Penzance people came up to Madron on the last bus to sleep with friends and relatives.

The Local Defence Volunteers were formed. At first this was little more than people like my dad, Charles Dale and Keeper Wooldridge sitting on Madron Carn watching for German parachutists. However, it soon became well organised as the Home Guard. Madron Home Guard was under the command of Captain Smith of Trelan. It was made up of two platoons, one under Harry

Harry Scrase's platoon at Trebean. Back row: B Cock, J Clemens, R Crocker, H Clemens, P Ansell, K Taylor, J Tuttle, N Walker; middle row: L Watts, C Curnow, H Scrase, P Jenkin, H Kent; front row: R Richards, J Ladner, A Roberts, F Dingle

Scrase and the other under Fred Berryman, and later, Jimmy Nicholls. They patrolled from Bull's View to Four Lanes End and from the Kennels to Lesingey Lane. Platoons took alternate nights, with half the platoon each night, meaning one night in four on duty. Guards slept at the workhouse, with two on patrol in rota. They stopped all traffic and looked out for suspicious people. They were armed with First World War Canadian 'Ross' rifles. These were delivered in two crates to Landithy Hall and were covered in grease. I remember spending many hours cleaning one for use. Manoeuvres took place on one Sunday each month. These usually involved one village acting as the enemy and attacking another. There were many humorous incidents. I will tell only one in which I was slightly involved.

Madron Home Guard were protecting Penzance from an attack by the Mousehole force. Mousehole were known to be approaching the village from Bull's View and were spotted entering the village. Jimmy Nicholls had his platoon in Tregoddick farmyard. He asked Basil Evans and myself to stand by the lower entrance to the pub and signal when they got to the post office. He had a homemade 'bomb' (like a giant firework) which he planned to lob over the cart

Fred Berryman's Patrol on the village green.
Back row: J Hall, A Nicholls, J Lawson, D Nicholls, L Williams, F Strick;
front row: L Prowse, J Nicholls, F Berryman, A Bidwell, W Eddy

shed as they came past the pub. We gave the signal and he threw his bomb.

Unfortunately it landed in the pub window and blew it in. Inside the window drinking his pint was George Matthews. He was covered in glass and beer and though only slightly injured was extremely irate. His language was sensational and the spectators fled.

An invasion was expected and all signposts were removed and village names blotted out. To the outsider Madron ceased to exist. One night in late 1940, the Home Guard were called out and told that the invasion had begun, but it turned out to be a false alarm. My mother hated having a gun in the house, so we kept it in the grandfather clock!

A Royal Observer Corps post was established on the Bull's View to Ding Dong road. There were numbers of air raid warnings and scattered bomb droppings, usually by single aircraft. Heamoor scout hall and Tregavarah chapel were destroyed. I was sitting outside our shop with some other boys watching a Dornier 'Flying Pencil' drop two bombs on Newlyn Harbour. Lord Haw Haw said that they had sunk a tanker. In fact they hit an old hulk where coal and fish oil were stored. The heaviest attack on Penzance came on 8 June 1941 when

Tregavarah Chapel, destroyed by a bomb in 1941

Poole's Brewery, Ruberry's Garage and Samuel the jewellers were destroyed. Another large bomb fell near the County School.

In order to protect Penzance, a heavy anti-aircraft battery was stationed in Madron Croft. There were four 3.7 guns, predictors and range finders together with 164 men. The guns and tents were across the valley from Madron playing field. The village did its best to entertain the troops. A canteen was started in the Men's Institute and dances were held regularly in Landithy Hall. Madron's younger women rejoiced in being so popular. The King William IV often ran out of beer. All entertainment was by local people. The Madron Concert Party led by Percy Jenkin, Fanny and Mary Pollard and Gella Rowe (later Maddern) were well known throughout West Cornwall. The best remembered dance was with the King's Own Regiment Dance Band. The Hall, yard and forecourt were packed and PC Kersey needed the help of four military police to keep control.

With the fire bomb attacks on British cities, Madron people were shown how to deal with incendiary bombs. Joe Stone and Ben Drew set up the Madron fire-watchers who patrolled from Mount View to the church during air raids.

When Plymouth was heavily bombed, Devonport High School children were evacuated to Penzance. At first many of them lived in Madron workhouse, but were later transferred to the Hotel Royale (Royal Court). Devonport High shared Penzance County School buildings. Local boys went to school from 9 am to 1 pm and Devonport from 1.30 pm until 5 pm.

In May 1942, Bill Cock and Frank Ansell returned to Madron after being bombed out of St Luke's College, Exeter. Numbers of Madron girls joined the Forces and Women's Land Army. Poltair and Trengwainton became Land Army hostels.

Madron people who wanted to swim in the sea could only do so locally from the small beach at Larrigan. The whole of the Eastern Green and Marazion beaches were covered in anti-invasion defences. In the summer of 1942 Basil Evans, Roderick Russell-Jones and I were on Larrigan beach when a German Focke-Wolfe fighter came in and machine gunned. We all dived into a trough in the beach but its target was inland. Geoff Russell Jones (Tregoddick Farm) was a fighter pilot and flew his Spitfire extremely low over Madron and the County School, waving to those below.

For Madron the most dangerous period of the war ended with the last raid on Penzance in September 1942. The Madron anti-aircraft guns fired in anger and hit a German bomber which crash landed at St Just. When the guns fired, the houses of Madron really shook and you could hear pieces of shrapnel dropping on roofs. This was the only occasion when we used our Morrison table shelter. The Madron church bells which, like all others, had been silent, only to be used as a sign of invasion, were rung to celebrate the victory of El Alamein.

1943 saw the arrival of American troops in Penzance, much to the delight of the younger local female population. They occupied a number of empty houses. On occasions they marched through Madron to manoeuvres on Madron Carn. There was an American ammunition dump near to the Carn and a GI sentry stood at the top gate. The American troops quickly found favour with the Poltair land girls, bringing them up to Madron pub. The more elderly Madron residents were shocked by the 'goings on'.

A number of British aircraft crash landed in the area. Early in the war a Beaufort medium bomber crashed on the present site of Mount's Bay School. One of the four crew was killed, the other three survived, badly injured. Local people were soon on the scene, the first being Arnold White. A Mosquito crashed near Lanyon Farm, spreading spent ammunition around the area. Gerald and Frank Williams, Tom Tucker and I collected a lot of cannonshell heads. Frank, who had started work in a Penzance garage, decided to make a cigarette lighter out of one shell head. While he was trying to file out a small protrusion, it exploded in the vice, pitting his face and hands with bits of metal. Tom Tucker and I took our bags of shellheads and threw them into the deepest of the flooded clay pits!

Later in the war a Beaufighter crashed at Bay of Biscay Farm, near Trythall School. Desmond Whiting and I ran up Break My Neck Lane and across fields to the farm. We could see the pilot trying to get out of the cockpit, but the hood was jammed. A soldier from the camp whom we knew jumped on the wing to try and help him. But the plane caught fire and ammunition began to explode. We Madron boys, peeping over a hedge were aghast to see a bullet cut across the soldier's neck, spilling blood. He fell back. Sadly, the pilot and navigator were burned to death.

The Homecoming Dinner for Madron's ex-servicemen. One Madron inhabitant wrote, 'Finally VE Day arrived with great jubilation and celebrations were soon organised. It was a great relief that the war was over. I can still see in my mind's eye the bonfire that was built on the village green. The blackouts were taken down and piled on top. Everyone was now waiting for those in uniform to be reunited with their loved ones.'

Throughout the war Madron had four shops. Miss Trembath's, at 3 Fore Street, sold milk and sweets. Our shop in Bill Cock's present front garden sold most of the rationed and general goods. Gella Rowe kept the Post Office in the present Boat House and an old lady called Barbara White kept the present shop which was not a Post Office and was far less busy. Knees was the largest toy shop in Penzance and there was a great shortage of toys. Mr Knee got Harry Scrase and Harry Kent to help him make children's wooden toys in William Richard's old farm just beyond the cemetery. These were well received and sold well.

The country was very short of food. Older children at village schools were given two weeks off school to pick up potatoes. It was hard work but the children enjoyed their small wages.

The government made great efforts to get the people to save National Savings to help the war effort. There was 'Spitfire Week', 'Warship Week' and 'Salute the Soldier Week'. Villages and towns vied with each other to raise the most money. The village people were very united in wartime. Everyone joined in. Colonel and Anne Bolitho attended all village functions, as did Mrs Le Grice.

Two Madron men deserted from the Forces and the local people were amused at P C Kersey's efforts to apprehend them. Both later returned to their units.

During the war there was a fear that there would be an epidemic of some sort. The isolation block at the workhouse was turned into the Isolation Hospital for West Cornwall. People with diphtheria and scarlet fever were sent there. The matron was a Mrs Turner.

Prior to the invasion of Normandy there was a great deal of activity in the area. The sky was filled with planes and the bay with ships. All Forces leave was cancelled. American troops left Penzance and there was a great shortage of men in West Cornwall. The Land Girls had to make do with the local teenage youths, surely a poor substitute! More and more victories were celebrated and an air of optimism grew. V E and V J days were greatly celebrated and everyone breathed a sigh of relief.

Madron men had served with distinction all over the world. Men had served with the 8th Army in the desert, in Italy, in Burma and France and Belgium. A few who should be mentioned were: Eddie Strick, who was a muleteer with Orde Wingate behind Japanese lines in Burma; Len Crocker, who sailed in tankers on Malta and Arctic convoys; Roy Crocker, who lost part of one hand a few days after the D-Day landings; and Teddy Lawrey, who joined the army as a boy soldier and fought the whole war on many fronts.

In October 1945, I left full time life in Madron to become a student at St Luke's College, Exeter.

Madron British Legion, formed about 1950 and now merged with Heamoor, where the British Legion Hall is to be found. Madron's banner is laid up in the church

Memorial House

Nurses

The Memorial House, Madron, was built in memory of those from the village who were killed in the Second World War. It was sited on land adjoining the Memorial Garden, provided by Trengwainton Estate, and has a beautiful outlook over Mount's Bay.

It was intended to house two district nurses, and its financial basis was admirably simple. Based on a public appeal, for every pound the parishioners raised, Colonel Edward Bolitho generously agreed to double the amount. (An Emily Bolitho House in Landithy Cottages, Churchtown, used to be home to a nurse in the parish in the early 1900s. In 1911 there was a health visitor, Edmund Barker, who stayed on in Madron for his retirement.)

The house was built soundly but with economy, re-using sinks, tiles and other materials available to the village, and was ready for occupation in 1952. It is believed that the first occupants were nurses Cook and Bailey, followed by nurses Start and Abbott.

Besides being a residence, the house had a waiting room and adjoining room intended as a clinic for expectant mothers, but as the health authorities came to disapprove of nurses living with their work the most that could be done was provide ante-natal relaxation exercises for up to four women at a time.

In 1957 Miss K Toms and Miss C Goldstone came to Madron as district nurses and midwives. Each had a large area to cover and, until 1966 when medical rules changed, twelve (not just one) doctors to work for. Nurse Goldstone covered Madron, Newmill, Newbridge, Bossullow, Morvah and Sancreed. Nurse Toms served Heamoor, Gulval, Nancledra, Halsetown and Boskenna. If they were away from the house they were required to leave a slate saying where they had gone in case they were needed urgently. There was no time for holidays!

Nurse Toms (left) and Nurse Goldstone

The following is a typical day in the life of the Madron district nurses, say 1965.

Before 9 am: housework, etc whilst taking telephone enquiries (anything from a baby's feeding problem to an old gentleman's ingrowing toenail).

9 am to lunch: rounds – diabetics; maternity work; surgical dressings; daily care of ill or old people; dirty dressings; any tuberculosis treatments.

Afternoon: blanket baths; health visiting, inclusive of all old people over 65, monthly or if necessary more often.

Also at regular intervals: school medical examinations, and women's relaxation classes.

Evening youth work at the Methodist church on Fridays (Miss Goldstone was the Methodist Sunday school superintendent); junior choir on Thursdays.

Nurse Toms and Nurse Goldstone looked after all the babies in the village and hamlets

To quote the nurses, both of whom are now retired and continue to live in Memorial House (today run by a trust), 'We had no time to be miserable!' Their enormous contribution to village life will always be warmly appreciated.

Farming in Madron

Buswarthen, Busiliack, Bosollow, Buswednan, Hendra, Landithy, Lanyon, Nanjeglos, Polteggan, Poltear, Trengwainton, Trewern, Trereife. Although the spelling has varied over the years, these lovely old Cornish farm names have endured through the ages and still remain today. However, in many cases it is only the name which survives: farms and farming have probably changed more than any other aspect of Madron's history.

In the earliest times people produced food solely to keep themselves alive. Gradually they found ways of producing crops and domesticating livestock, and this led to the formation of the early settlements, to Chysauster and Carn Euny for example, which were the forerunners of the modern farms.

Agriculture slowly progressed and farmers produced food for sale. The work was hard and involved the whole family, as much labour was needed to plant and harvest crops. A few cows for milking by hand, cattle for fattening and pigs

Farming in 1910 – ploughing (above) and a threshing machine (below)

Above: Threshing at Landithy

Below: An elevator at work at Tregoddick

Above: The end of the day at Tregoddick (Aldreath House in the background)

Below: Gathering seaweed at Penzance, to be applied as fertiliser to the fields at Trebean

Above: An interval in hay baling – time for croust, about 1960

Below: Pre-war freesia picking at Trebean Nurseries. Trebean was already a nursery when Methuselah Watts from Scilly purchased the property in 1902. In its heyday the nursery employed a dozen people growing freesias, daffodils, irises and tomatoes

Ralph Tomlin of Polgoon Farm, on the watch for any disease in his daffodils

were also reared. Produce would be taken around the neighbourhood and sold direct to customers.

In the 18th century on the small family farms of the parish, wage earning labourers were few and pauper children, who lived in, were often apprenticed to farmers by the parish overseers. Fields averaged three acres in size and were protected by Cornish hedges of stone. The soil was acid and gravelly, supporting

Sorting daffodil bulbs at Trereife

bracken and heather. Large tracts of peat were cut for winter fuel on the highest moors and in May large flocks and herds of beasts were brought up to graze from the lowlands. Native cattle were black, small and hardy. Gaunt work horses were kept and numbers of coarse-woolled, half-wild sheep roamed about freely with identifying marks. Thousands of geese were reared for the markets.

With the gradual improvement in crop husbandry, yields improved, markets were established and farming in the area flourished. Broccoli, spring greens, potatoes and flowers were grown; every farm had a few acres of each. From Victorian times onwards much of the produce went to 'upcountry' markets by train (road transport has now largely taken over). With the formation of the Milk Marketing Board in 1933 farmers were able to supply the Creamery at St Erth, which processed the milk and distributed it all over the country. Livestock for sale would be taken to Penzance cattle market. Sadly, despite moving from the old site at the top of Causewayhead (now two car parks) to a purpose built site at Long Rock, this closed in 1999.

Of the 41 farms in the parish with a value of over £10 in 1768, only six remain as holdings used solely for agricultural purposes. Many have been amalgamated. In one case, seven of the originals are now farmed as one unit.

Continuous farming over at least the last 5000 years has created the historic landscape for which West Penwith is famous. The formation of the West Penwith Environmentally Sensitive Area (ESA) in 1987 has now preserved this landscape. The small stone-hedged fields and the unimproved moorland are a testimony to the generations of men and women who have worked this land.

Madron Young Farmers Club

The club can trace its origins back to late 1937 when at a meeting in Landithy Hall, held as a result of a Cornwall County Education Committee initiative, it was decided to form a Madron Young Farmers Club (YFC). The ambitious programme included farm walks, lectures, visits to agricultural businesses, and experiments with the raising of calves and pigs. When, after a wartime break, the club was re-formed in 1949, John Uren and Lennox Green were founder members.

Over the years many thousands of pounds have been raised for local charities. Dung bagging and ploughing marathons seemed to be the main events for fund raising, not forgetting, however, the famous carol singing, about which malicious rumours say that most people paid them to stay away rather than hear their vocal efforts!

YFC has faced many ups and downs since 1937, probably following the fortunes of farming, but continues today with the same enthusiasm and friendship it has always had.

No one knows why but Madron YFC has always been successful in public speaking competitions. On several occasions they have held all the county trophies for both senior and junior titles. Members have then gone on to represent the county and the south west nationally. Here (1975) are J Wallis, S Dennis, F Rowley, A Skewes, unknown, M Pengelly

Lennox Green and his family at Bosullow. In his many years there, he farmed about 65 acres, keeping typically 18 dairy cows and 48 beef cattle, as well as fattening 4000 pigs annually. The account of Bossullow's history has been contributed by Mr Green

Bossullow

This hamlet lies to the north-west of Madron village near the border with Morvah, sheltering under the high moors which run east to west from St Ives to Land's End.

Among the earliest recorded landlords of Bossullow, named on an 1845 map, were Mrs Praed, John Batten Esq., Mr Saundry, the Earl of Falmouth, GW Gregory Esq., Samuel Borlase, and William Rashleigh.

The original names of the very old properties were Bossullow Lane End, Bossullow Vean, Bossullow Veor, Great Bossullow Barton, Trehyllis (Old Bossullow) and Little Bossullow.

Until about ten years ago Bossullow was a self-contained unit with its own chapel and school. There were two Wesleyan places of worship in Little Bossullow: the first, with an ash and cinder floor, was built in approximately 1760; the second was built in 1845. The first one proved to be too small and became the Sunday schoolroom. In the second chapel the women sat on the left-hand side and men on the right. In 1880 the Sunday school records show 100 scholars, four superintendents, who were fined 4 d. for absence, 17 teachers and four secretaries, whose absence incurred a 2 d. fine.

Mr Saundry of St Levan, the owner of the land on which the 1845 chapel was built, granted a lease of 999 years. In 1865 he sold the site of the Sunday school for the princely sum of £6. The 1845 chapel was not solemnized for marriages until 1978 when by a special temporary arrangement the one and only marriage took place of Deborah Mary Lennox Green. Although the chapel closed in 1991, a service of blessing was held in 1995 for Deborah's sister Olivia Ruth Squire Green who married Alan Blake. Both chapel and Sunday school are listed buildings, now converted into a large residence.

There have been two day schools in the hamlet. The first opened in Great Bossullow, circa 1836, but became too small (many miners lived at Bossullow then) and closed in 1882. It was converted into a farm building in about 1990. The second, and larger school beside the Madron to Morvah road, opened in 1882 – the date can be seen cut in the granite above a window. This school closed in 1990 and was converted into a dwelling, and is now the Mên-an-Tol Studio.

Great Bossullow farmhouse originally had a thatched roof, but when the 1845 chapel was being built with a slate roof, the owners decided to follow suit with a slate replacement.

Bossullow hamlet lies in the midst of a number of ancient monuments cut from the rough local granite: West Lanyon Quoit, Lanyon Cromlech, Mên-an-Tol, the Four Parishes Rock, Mên Scryfa, Chûn Castle, Chûn Quoit and Trehyllis settlement/village to the east of Chûn Castle and as yet unexcavated.

Water was vital to the community and hence there were three public wells: Kerrow Well – an open well – and Great Bossullow Well were hedged around

Lennox Green at the 1845 Chapel

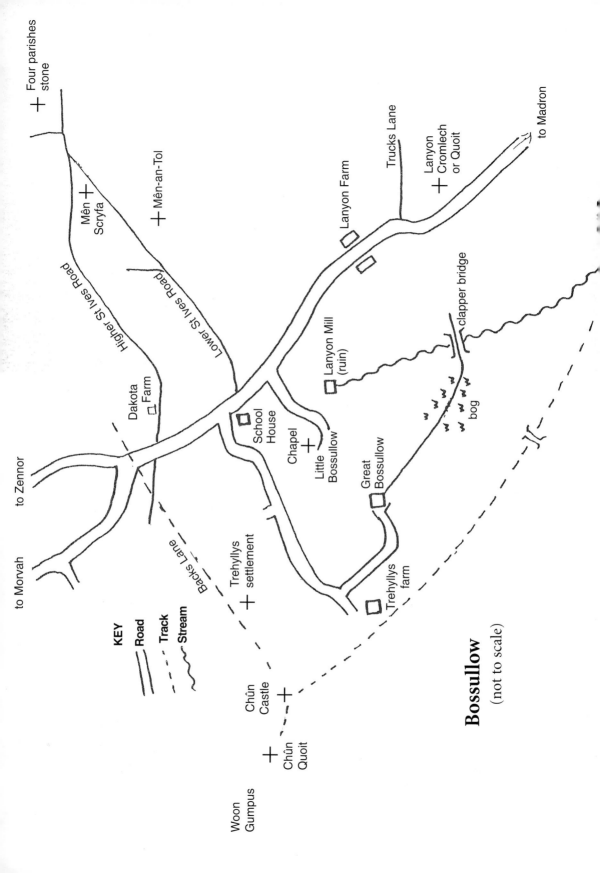

Four parishes stone

to Zennor

to Morvah

Higher St Ives Road

Lower St Ives Road

Mên Scryfa

Mên-an-Tol

Dakota Farm

School House

Chapel

Little Bossullow

Great Bossullow

Lanyon Mill (ruin)

Lanyon Farm

Trucks Lane

Lanyon Cromlech or Quoit

to Madron

clapper bridge

bog

Trehyllys settlement

Trehyllys farm

Backs Lane

Chûn Castle

Chûn Quoit

Woon Gumpus

KEY

Road

Track

Stream

Bossullow

(not to scale)

Corn mows at Bossullow, about 1960

and had an iron gate entrance; another was at Little Bossullow. Chûn Castle, an Iron Age fortress built over 200 metres above sea level, also needed water and sure enough within its central ring is an excellent shallow well, never known to run dry.

There are many interesting field names in the area, one worthy of mention being Shop Field near Lanyon Bridge where there was once a blacksmith's shop nearby. This blacksmith rejoiced in the splendid name of Melchizedek Phillips (1797-1883). He was a trustee of both Bossullow chapels and is interred in Madron churchyard. Another interesting field name is Butcher's Corner, opposite the Mên-an-Tol studio. According to legend, the giant Helebron who lived at St Michael's Mount came regularly to this field to play pitch and toss with the huge rocks.

The Lanyon river, which rises in the area between Ding Dong Mine and the Mên-an-Tol, flows down to the Drift dam. This provided ample water for several mills on its course. Lanyon Mill was near Little Bossullow and was said to consist in fact of two mills, one milling produce for human consumption, the other, for livestock feed. Adjoining was a house for the miller and for a skilled millwright engineer. It was the scene of a tragic accident in 1940 when the miller, Robert Penberthy, was caught by his jacket in the cogs and crushed, killing him instantly. The mill never worked again and many will remember the moving service held for Robert Penberthy at Bossullow Wesley.

Fireball damage at Bossullow, 1937

Another disaster occurred at Bossullow in 1937. Miners leaving work at Geevor at about 3 am one day were amazed to see a ball of fire heading in from the sea and crossing Woon Gumpus before hitting Bossullow, severely damaging the two Kerrow farmhouses and all the farm buildings. Miraculously no one was injured and the strange phenomenon died out harmlessly in the Carfury area. Fortunately the property was adequately insured and a large number of builders worked for weeks restoring all the buildings.

Once there was a cart track from Great Bossullow eastwards, providing the shortest route to Madron and Penzance. It crossed the Lanyon river over a clapper bridge consisting of four granite rocks, and was much used by pack horses.

Carved on the rocks are the initials 'JHW' and 'WE' and the date '1864'. Approaching the bridge from the west is a very dangerous bog and to make it safe for wagons a paved granite causeway was constructed across it for about 150 yards. Sadly, now overgrown with bracken, brambles and sedge grass, the track and bridge are hard to locate.

Today there are about twenty houses in this attractive hamlet set amid its fascinating ancient monuments and its panoramic views beneath tremendous skies.

Boswarthen

This little hamlet, a couple of miles or so to the north-west of Madron, is near the ancient Well and Baptistry. The 1841 census tells us that six families were living there:

1. William Andrews, a miner aged 40, his wife and eight children.
2. James Dale, aged 80, his wife and two children.
3. Charles Friggens, farmer and widower aged 72, his son, a farmer, and his wife and four young children plus two servants. (The present Madron family of Friggens, as far as is known, have no relationship with this Friggens family.)
4. Thomas Pascoe, a tin dresser aged 30, his wife and four children.
5. James Mann, an agricultural labourer aged 70, his wife and three children, one of whom was a tin dresser.
6. John Matthews, a farmer aged 50, his wife and ten children, of whom the eldest son, William, was a farmer.

In 1920 there were six farms and one cottage at Boswarthen. Ben Thomas farmed Lower Boswarthen's 75 acres from 1920 until 1950 when his son Harold took over the tenancy. Tommy Davey's farm was 50 acres and the other four

An aerial view of Boswarthen

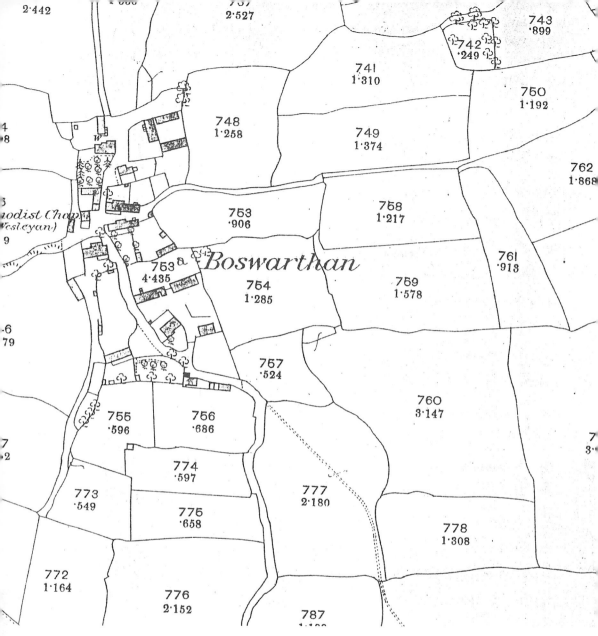

Boswarthen as it appears on the Ordnance Survey map of 1878

were smallholdings. Each farm had its own well (peeth). A spring in a meadow near Bull's View filled cattle troughs before winding its way to the Kennel river.

Dairying was the main business of the farms. Harold Thomas remembers his herd of Guernseys and his father supplying milk to the workhouse, delivered by a horse and trap, whilst eggs, milk and butter were taken down to Penzance to be sold in the market. In later years potatoes and broccoli were grown, especially during the Second World War.

As the motor age dawned in West Penwith dairy items were taken down to market by car, that is after Ben Thomas had learned to control one of the new fangled machines. Harold tells how one was brought out to Boswarthen to his dad for approval and possible purchase. After a few preliminary circuits around a meadow, Ben was told he was all right to drive and he did so. Unfortunately he hadn't quite mastered braking and to everyone's dismay he failed to stop at the closed field gate but with a splintering crash charged straight through it!

As regards the buildings in Boswarthen not much is known of their age, though the farmhouse where Tommy Davey lived has '1676', together with the letters 'SM', carved into the granite on the front. For many years there was a Wesleyan chapel in the hamlet, but this must have become redundant for it was sold in about 1902 to help pay for Madron's new Methodist chapel. In Harold Thomas's time it was used as an implement shed. The small school that once operated at Boswarthen also disappeared and the children walked either to Madron or to Trythall for their schooling.

So this little hamlet, which for so long had been largely self-sufficient, lost its independence and in 1987 all the farms were amalgamated into one worked by Stuart Nicholls and his son. The old chapel and other buildings and barns have been converted into living accommodation.

West Lanyon

This deserted medieval settlement was excavated by the late E Marie Minter and members of the Cornwall Archaeological Society in 1964. Known as Old Lanyon, it lies approximately 450 metres south-west of the present Lanyon Farm. At that time its presence was denoted by the high standing walls of two long houses, a barn and garden enclosures seen easily enough in winter and

*The deserted
medieval settlement
of West Lanyon*

Lanyon Thomas and his family at Lanyon Farm, where he was born and spent his working life

spring. Its name was recorded in 1214 as Liniein, in 1244 Linyeine and in 1326 Lyneyn, meaning in Cornish 'lynn = pool: yeyn= cold'. Pottery found during excavation was consistent with constant use of the site from the 13th up to the end of the 17th centuries. It belonged to the manor of Binnerton.

By 1390 the main settlement at Lanyon was at or near the present farm. In 1770 Philip Rashleigh as owner of Lanyon was paying a high rent to Sir John St Aubyn as Lord of Binnerton. Eventually, in 1908 Lanyon passed from Rashleigh hands into the ownership of Thomas Robins Bolitho whose family continue to own it. The Bone family currently farm there as tenants.

The Western Hunt

In a 1780 diary relating to Madron parish is a record that 'William Veal of Trevaylor in the adjoining parish of Gulval sold a pack of harriers to Sir Rose Price of Trengwainton for 14 guineas.' These were hunted on three days a week, in the mornings only. In 1785 John Easterbrook became huntsman, receiving 5 guineas a year. The last of Sir Rose Price's huntsmen, named Coombs, lived in the small cottage by the Sportsman's Arms, Heamoor. The adjoining 'Carman's Yard' was the site of the kennels. This marked the beginning of the Western Hunt.

In 1784 several young hounds are named along with those who walked them:

'Forrester' at Rosemorran – Mr Peter Woolcocks
'Ruby' at Ridgeovean – Mr G Fox
'Tipsy' at Boskednan – Mr W Saundry

Followers at this time included: Captain Goodman, William Jelbart, William Corin, Mr Fox, Naylon Vinscombe, James Trembath, R Phillips, Thos. Trenery, Wm Friggens, Mr Eddy, Thomas Treloar and John James. After Sir Rose Price's mastership ended, hunting continued in an informal, loosely organised way for some years with various people, such as the Le Grices, running packs of hounds

The Western Hunt at the lodge entrance, Trengwainton, 1930-31

On the way to the Boxing Day meet, 2000

for a few years, then selling them on to other interested parties. Penwith was shared out at any one time among these 'informal' huntsmen and there were 'interesting' confrontations at times when packs arrived to hunt over the same farm!

In 1863 hunting became established in the area by the Bolitho family with a recognised pack and Master of Foxhounds, and this was confirmed when Trengwainton was purchased in 1866. In about 1890 the present premises in

The Hunt kennels, 2000

Kennel Lane were built and the cottage hard by was associated with it until it was sold off in the 1970s.

The Western Hunt today operates over the whole area to the west of a line drawn from Portreath to Porthleven. Madron's view of it usually comes from the two traditional meets in the village, one on Boxing Day when the sharing of the stirrup cup is a welcome treat on a fine, brisk morning – and the other on the Monday of the Feast.

The hunt also provides other tangible services to the community, including helping people in its pony club with their riding, teaching them how to handle a horse safely. In addition it assists farmers by removing dead animals. Originally the idea was that the animals would provide food for the hounds, but circumstances have changed, especially after it became illegal in 1966 to send calves (bull calves mostly) to France for veal. Today bull calves are worth little or no money, so the hunt's help in their disposal has become a significant contribution for farmers.

Still a part of traditional village and rural life, the hunt continues but is now beset with doubts and uncertainties. Ben Sparrow, the Master, is both quietly confident and resigned to whatever may emerge in the future. Ed Bailey, the kennel huntsman, plus the part-time helpers hope their livelihoods will be preserved and that their hounds will continue to lead the lives for which they have been bred and trained.

Village characters

In a row of thatched cottages pulled down and replaced by Landithy Hall in 1909 lived a little old lady remembered for her eccentricity. She kept a stuffed peacock on the stairs and had a grand piano on which her chickens roosted.

Other characters living around the turn of the 20th century were:

Thomas Cock, the sexton, feared by all the children for his ferocity of countenance and who brought water to the village in dry summers from Nanceglos and sold it to the drought-stricken villagers. His donkey, Abraham, and cart with no springs were sometimes hired to take children on days' outings for a shilling.

Billy Jenkin, the smith and master of the bell ringers, also the village constable, kept the Ding Dong miners' tools sharp. Once, he was taking a prisoner to Bodmin by horse and trap. The man escaped but Billy 'caught 'un, wrassled 'un to the ground', and sat on his beard until help came!

Jane Pengelly was a serving maid at Landithy Farm. She reputedly used to sit on kegs of smuggled brandy, spreading her skirts over them while preventive

Harry Scrase's Austin 7 during the war, dubbed 'The Flying Bedstead'. Harry was the first to bring welding to the area, with a workshop near the old Ritz Cinema, Penzance

officers searched the house.

William Richards lived with his mother at a village shop and farmed a small holding. He fetched sand from Hayle with his horse and cart which his mother sold in 1/2d. and pennyworths to the cottagers who used it to sand their floors.

Harry Scrase was well known to an older generation and much involved in village life. He was affectionately linked to his Austin 7 which he ran from 1930 through to the '50s. It was one of only about four cars in Madron during the early post-war period, and in due course little of the original remained, but it was kept going by 'spares' from his Penzance workshop. On one occasion he welded an old bedstead to the chassis. The car had many names, including the Madron Fire Engine when painted black with flame red wings, and Royal Lash up after its 'RL' registration. It had a number of community uses too – as lookout post for Madron Home Guard, container of gas for balloons on Madron Carn during George VI celebrations, and ice cream cart during celebrations at the end of World War II. Harry always claimed it never let him down on Madron Hill and, unbelievably, even squeezed eleven children and seven adults into it from time to time!

Joe Bryant was elderly in 1945. He had a gold nugget on his watch chain, hav-

'The Flying Bedstead' on Zig Zag Hill, during the Trengwainton Hill Climb

ing mined in Canada with at least two other Madron men – John Curnow and Andrew Friggens. Joe used to love to say to youngsters, 'Do 'ee want to see gold, boy?' Then he would flourish the nugget before their wide eyes. He was also a rather eccentric cricket umpire.

Mr and Mrs T J Cock were born in Madron and lived there all their lives They kept the village store, retiring in 1959. Before her marriage Mrs Cock (née Agnes Leggo) had been a teacher at the Daniel school from the age of 14. She was a founder member in 1918 of Madron WI and its first treasurer. Both she and Mr Cock were from very old Madron families.

Mr T J Cock and his wife (née Agnes Leggo) from two very old Madron families – back in the early 1600s another Agnes Leggo had married a John Cock

Brian Wallis (left) and a copper dish made by him. He worked in copper inlaid with pewter, brass, stainless steel and silver, and his work was commissioned from Norway to Kuwait. When not beating copper he thumped the leather ball for Madron Cricket Club

Brian Wallis lived with his sister, Mrs Kanga Parsons, at Kennel Cottage where he made hand-beaten copper bowls, trays and mirrors. He came from Cheshire in 1962 where he had learned his craft from his father.

Mr Stevens' blacksmith's shop at Newmill had been established for about 50

Mr Stevens' blacksmith's shop at Newmill

Above: Madron's blacksmith's shop, with (left to right) Dick Maddern, Billy Jenkin, lad Walter Nicholls, Percy Jenkin, Ben Thomas and blacksmith Horace Jenkin

Below: Moreton Giles, an ex-serviceman with the RAF, ran an agricultural engineering works from 1947 in what had been the village smithy. He was rarely seen without his cheroot and restored many a damaged car to good health. He was a bachelor, interested in good food and golf

Sam Richards was a lay reader in the parish and the longest serving reader in the county. By profession he was a chemist, travelling by early morning train to Truro each day. He was also an expert at crocheting, which fascinated fellow passengers. He came to live at Tregoddick Cottages and this is where he died

years in 1965. Although smiths were disappearing from the country scene they found plenty of work, mostly shoeing hunters and ponies. Mr Stevens lived at Kitty Noye's cottage near the smithy.

Ted Ford, when an amateur photographer, won several photographic competitions. His most treasured possession then was a letter of congratulation from Mr Archie Parker, the Royal Photographer. Now he is a professional, specialising in wedding photographs.

Tom Semmens lived in Tregoddick Cottages and was rarely seen without his pipe of twist. He'd been a quarryman in his earlier years, walking each day to Penlee or Castle an Dinas. Later he worked at Landithy

The handbell ringers, a group which flourished in the early 1970s

Handbell ringers

Recollections by Sally Westren (née Friggens) and Susan Dann

The group was formed in the early 1970s with encouragement and enthusiasm from the then vicar of Madron, the Reverend Bill Rowett. For many years there had been a set of handbells in the parish, but they had rarely been used. We youngsters enjoyed taking up the challenge to become handbell ringers and had weekly meetings which helped us develop our skills.

Within a short space of time a 'noise' was produced which resembled a tune. This encouraged the group greatly and with perseverance we became an established and confident band of ringers. Our debut was in the parish of Madron, but it was not long before our fame spread and we were invited to entertain at various local venues. One honour bestowed on the group was an invitation to ring our bells in the church tent at the Royal Cornwall Show.

Our reputation and experience were growing and the Reverend Rowett felt we were ready to spread our wings further. For the next two years he entered us in the South West Region's Federation of Handbell Ringers Annual Festival. The weekends away were great fun and Bill Rowett deserved praise both for organising them and for his bravery in taking a group of noisy and excited teenagers away.

Our time in the group was happy and fulfilling, and looking back it was clearly an important and rewarding part of our youth. Naturally, we eventually grew up and moved on but other handbell teams followed. When Bill Rowett left the parish there was no other leader about who had the commitment and charisma to keep things going. The bells were returned to their box and have only rarely been aired since. For the present they remain part of Madron's history – a dormant force waiting to be used again!

Floats at the Silver Jubilee festivities in 1977

The Chapel float – 'Harvest home'

The WI float – 'Women through the ages'

Queen Elizabeth's silver jubilee, 1977

Plans had been made well in advance to celebrate this occasion in fine style. In school, children received a silver jubilee badge, as did all Sunday school children not yet at school in January. Fund raising events took place, culminating in July in a grand carnival procession which was supported by everyone in the village. There were so many walkers and floats that as the first reached Heamoor the last were just leaving the assembly point. They processed all the way to Penzance Promenade, the walkers returning by special bus and rejoining the floats at the George V Memorial Field.

Here the children received silver jubilee mugs. Sports and games were held – pillow fights on greasy poles, a tug of war between men and women. And there were also teas, a band playing and other happenings which all contributed to a grand village occasion.

Above: One of the highlights was an evening cricket match in which cross-dressing featured prominently

Below: Bill Cock, Master of Ceremonies

Gymnastics at a summer fête in the school playground, 1930s

Summer fêtes

These are a long established event in Madron's history, although no definite records occur until 1946. The fête that year was due to be held at Landithy Meadow in August, but a heavy storm caused it to be moved to the hall, prompting the comment, 'Things always go with a bang at Madron!' It was nevertheless successful and graceful gymnastics were performed by the ladies.

Rationing was still in force in 1948 when at Trengwainton there were 13 stalls. One displayed items made by a working party to be sold 'coupon free'. A concert was given by the Madron Players, and the children took part in country dancing and maypole dancing. In all they raised £350 9s. 9d. So many goods were left over that St Thomas Church took them for their October bazaar at Heamoor.

In the 1950s Judge Scobell Armstrong and Mrs Armstrong hosted the fête at their Nancealverne home for several years, during which bowling for a pig became popular. Later it moved to the Vicarage House grounds.

During the 1980s two notable fêtes were held. In 1982 St Thomas and Madron churches joined forces and used the Vicarage Cottage to display church records, plate, silver, prints, photographs and documents. In 1983, when Reverend Gilbert was vicar, the highlight of the day was a display of Red Indian

The summer fête moved to the Vicarage House grounds (now the Old Vicarage) when Reverend David Cox was vicar. Here he is seen with Mr C Le Grice and Mrs Shearer who opened the fête in the late 1960s

dancing by members of the Peace Pipe Lodge from Hayle, dressed in authentic costumes. During 1988-93 fêtes were held at Bellair House by invitation of Mr and Mrs Russell Whitlock, and during the mid 90s in the vicarage garden and hall. The school now provides the venue for the summer fêtes, in July.

Later snapshots

In November 1986 a special function was held to highlight the consecration of the church in 1336. 650 years after this original consecration 'Landithy Manor Hall' was suitably decorated with medieval banners, shields and weapons, and 14th-century music was played in the background. As guests arrived they were handed warm punch by serving wenches and jesters. Candlelit tables were spread with refreshments consisting of bread, cheese, hog's pudding and a choice of wines.

Frank Warnes described the village scene as it might have been at the time – the church with a tower only half its present height, a dusty lane leading to the blacksmith's shop, the vicar's dwelling near to where Landithy Farm stands today and the adjacent hospital of the Knights of St John, a lodging house for travellers. The village folk and those from surrounding homesteads, women dressed mainly in brown kersey or sackcloth, men in belted tunics and well behaved children under the watchful eye of the respected parson, William of Beverley.

In the Old Vicarage grounds stands Vicarage Cottage. When the Reverend R Gilbert was the incumbent in the Vicarage during its last five years of use (1981-86) the cottage was controlled by the Glebe Committee.

Mr H Tutt, who celebrated his 90th birthday in January 1992, came to live in Vicarage Cottage after the death of his wife. He arrived in Penzance during the war to work for the Western Union Telegraph Company, but in addition he worked tirelessly for the well being of Madron church buildings in practical ways and throughout the long interregnum served as a churchwarden. He also organised lesson readers and sidesmen's rotas for thirty years until old age finally forced him to give up.

When Vicarage Cottage again became vacant it was made available to the parish for meetings, whist drives, handbell ringers and a playgroup run by Miss Sally Friggens. A concrete path was laid by Mr R White and Mr T Furlong so that dry access could be had. Furniture, floor coverings and crockery for the kitchen were all donated and the various rooms were used by several organisations. The cottage stands there still.

The playing field

King George's Field, Madron, is home to Madron Football Club, Madron Women's Football Club, Alverton Athletica Football Club under 10s, Penzance Cricket Club and Gulval Cricket Club. It sprang to life in 1938 when in March of that year Lieutenant Colonel Edward Bolitho generously gave the field to the National Playing Field Association (NPFA) for use as a recreation ground for the village. A children's playground was also set up together with entrance gates mounted on stone pillars in Aldreath Road.

The opening of the Pavilion in 1961

A 1950s cricket team

The field was managed by a committee of management trustees of which Mr Bill Cock was secretary for 46 years until his retirement in 1994 when he was awarded a 'Golden Torch' by the NPFA in recognition of his magnificent service.

The present pavilion, a splendid effort of voluntary labour, was opened in 1961, ensuring that for many years the facilities at Madron were among the best in Penwith. Unfortunately it is now showing its age, but having gone through a dark period things are looking rosier with field affairs. With grant aid, the children's playground has been renovated to NPFA standards and the committee is actively investigating sources of funding for the pavilion. There is an air of quiet confidence in the outcome.

Madron Cricket Club

The mellow sound of leather on willow has been a lively feature of Madron's sporting life for well over a century.

In the early 1900s Madron teams were playing in the same county league as Penzance on one of Colonel Bolitho's fields near Home Farm, Trengwainton. The colonel was a keen player in his younger days and he saw to it that teas were properly provided in one of the adjoining barns. In 1907 the village possessed a strong eleven who beat the Devon and Cornwall Light Infantry who were stationed in the village for their annual training.

The 1st XI of 1968, winners of the Cooke Cup. Back row: Francis Monk (umpire), Ben Ladner, Claude Semmens, Lesley Jenkin, Alan Lawrence, Bill Cock, Ken Tregarthen, Philip Eddy, Gordon Matthews (umpire). Front row: Jim Matthews, Keith Boase, Sydney Hall (President), Desmond Whiting, John Evans, Ervin Young, David Boase, Vivian Pengelly (with cup)

Later the club moved to a large field near the White Gate, situated on the left of the main road just before the turning to Boswarthen and the Baptistry. There was no facility for heating water at the wooden pavilion, so this vital commodity was carried in a large tea urn from nearby 'Polclose', lived in at that time by the Scrase family.

In those pre-Hitler war days, Mr Lockhart lived at 'Skeldar', behind Tregoddick Farm, and he was a great supporter of the village club. It is a fact very little known generally that he occasionally invited down to stay two friends whose fame in the cricket world could scarcely be surpassed – namely the great, great Jack Hobbs and the renowned Herbert Strudwick of Surrey and England. Whether they ever appeared under A N Other in the MCC side (Madron Cricket Club of course) is a matter of mere speculation!

No competitive cricket was played during the First World War and afterwards, when the club was revived, the playing area was moved to the King George V playing field alongside the football pitch. The first secretary of the post war club was Mr Bill Friggens, the first skipper was Tom Nicholls and some of their star players were Bill Semmens, Charlie Hollow, John Reed (head of the village school) and Jack Tonkin. A great deal of hard work was put into improving the playing area which was ploughed up, levelled and re-seeded. Chiefly involved were Sydney Hall, Jack Maddern, Leonard Jenkin and Brian Wallis. Due to their efforts, the cricket square became one of the best for junior clubs in the area.

The Cooke Cup, competed for by junior cricket clubs throughout Cornwall, is a good yardstick by which to judge the success of a club. Madron began its climb to fame modestly enough. We hear little of their exploits for a few years, only that the club was not represented in the associated Runciman Cup due to 'unreliable batting'! But after running out as winners in the West Penwith League in 1951 and the evening league in 1956, they had their first Cooke Cup success in 1959, sharing the trophy with Four Lanes. In 1960 they convincingly defeated Perran-ar-Worthal in the final at Troon. The main feature of this game was an unbroken opening stand between Tom Pollard and Gerald Semmens. The side was skippered by Bill Cock. In 1962 Madron shared the trophy with Perran-ar-Worthal and in 1967 and '68 won it outright under the captaincy of Desmond Whiting. Some of the outstanding cricketers of this period were Charlie Hollow, Ervin Young and Sydney Hall, with the help of a very strong squad of players, mostly from the village.

Bearing this level of enthusiasm and achievement in mind it is encouraging to learn that after a prolonged lapse Madron Cricket Club is being revived and that 2001 sees the beginning of that welcome development.

Soccer in Madron

Soccer has been played in Madron for far longer than anyone can remember. Teams have represented the village for much longer than there are records of the game. But we do know that, after the playing field was given to the village in 1935 by Colonel E Bolitho to celebrate King George V's Silver Jubilee, football flourished in its new secure home. A large wooden shed was provided for the players' use and served for many years before the present pavilion was built in 1961 by a co-operative effort on the men's part, the driving force behind which was Jackie Maddern, a player and well-known builder.

After the Second World War the game was tremendously popular and the village ran a first and a second team. The first eleven, known as the Gunners, played in the West Penwith League, the Hospital Cup and the Charity Cup. The seconds played for the Heamoor Shield. Red and white striped top and white

Above: A pre-war Madron soccer team. Note the mascot

Below: The first team of 1948-49. Back row: G Williams, G Semmens, Goalkeeper Kent, E Matthews; middle row: J Matthews, C Hollow, W Nicholls, W W Cock, T Pollard; front row: F Strick, J Cummings

'The Stiffs', 1948-49. Back row: T Day, T Tucker, T Furlong, G Semmens; middle: M Laity, E Matthews, G Ellis, P Matthews, D Nicholls; front: D Whiting, J Maddern

shorts were the first team's strip, whilst the second team had red tops, white collars and white shorts, and were affectionately known as the Stiffs. Both teams wore the Lanyon Quoit emblem on their shirts and blazers.

Transport for away matches was provided by Joan Berryman's milk float and if Joan was unable to go Walter Nicholls drove. Later on, Donnithorne Taxis transported the first team. First team players paid two shillings per match, while the second team paid one shilling. At this time the club president was Mr RW Smith of Trelan.

Teams played against included Mousehole, St Levan (for whom Ronnie George was a feared opponent), St Buryan (whose Freddie Phillips went on to greater things with Penzance and the county side), St Just, Pendeen, Ludgvan and Marazion. But Madron men have been farther afield, over the Tamar and up to the Home Counties where on a tour they played Thames Valley and even the mighty Kingstonians whom they held to a memorable 3-3 draw.

In recent times Madron has reached new heights of success. In the 1998-99 season they made a clean sweep of all the trophies on offer in the West Penwith League. They were not only league champions but also won the Hanneford Cup, the Nicholas Cup, the Penzance & District Charity Cup and the West Cornwall Hospital Cup. And they continue to sweep all before them.

Wrestling

Though the art of wrestling is now sadly in decline, Madron men once had renowned Cornish wrestlers in their midst. Friggens and Trezise won the gold and silver laced caps in a match which took place in 1828 in Penzance (then in the parish). It lasted three days and was watched by 3000 spectators who had come from miles around to see the contests.

Although the sport was common throughout England as early as the 15th century and most counties had their own individual style of wrestling, it was always followed with particular passion in Cornwall. Cornishmen are said to have fought under a banner of two wrestlers at Agincourt.

Madron's growth

During the medieval period Madron was a small community – Churchtown, established around the church, the pubs and the blacksmith's shop. Premises between the present shop towards the church were thatched in the 1880s.

Tregoddick was lived in by some vicars prior to the vicarage (now the Old Vicarage) being built; it also served as a lodging house for visiting clergy. The house between the shop and the chapel was the last one that Mrs R Bolitho had built. Unfortunately she died before its completion, leaving her nephew with the task of finishing it. He called it Folnamodry – aunt's folly.

The strange, prow-shaped house on the corner of Aldreath Road was known as the Boat House. It had supposedly been used as a smuggler's cottage, although its precise use is unknown. The parish council used to give an annual Poor Man's Dinner there, costing 1s. 6d.

One of the oldest original houses in Fore Street has the date 1828 carved on its lintel. Penmont, 1886, opposite the King William IV, once served as the parish council offices and reading rooms. It was accessed by outside steps at the back. At one time there was a rifle range behind Landithy Hall; now it has been demolished. Down by Landithy Farm huge dumps of stone were stored by stone workers to fill holes in the roads.

In 1946 T G Olds was at Vicarage Cottage advertising as a radio engineer for battery radios and also electrical installations. W Allen of Churchtown was a carpenter and undertaker, and Friggens Bros, carpenters and joiners, lived at Holly Cottage offering painting, decorating and general maintenance. Milk was delivered by Berryman and White, tomatoes and flowers were available at Trebean, and there was a cobbler, Hedley Harris, at the back of Tarbean's yard.

Prior to 1949 water came to the village from the Wishing Well, through pipes to pumps and taps across to Landithy Farm, feeding two pumps, one near the chapel on Fore St (the tank was in waste ground nearby), the other near Penmont where the council notice board is situated. There were shutes at Landithy Hall, 1909; at Far End and above the chapel (later tapped); a tap at the

The village smithy, on the corner of Fore Street and Aldreath Road

Left: Pump by the Chapel   Right: Originally a shute, now tapped, outside Landithy Hall

cemetery; a pump in Aldreath Road at Vingoes Row (now demolished) and the shute at Nanceglos near Trengwainton. In a hot summer if the pumps ran dry, people went down Nanceglos Hill to the shute for a barrel of water because this one never ran dry.

In February 1949 the vicar wrote the following in his parish notes: 'Madron as a village may look very picturesque to those who pass through it. To those who know it well however, things are not always what they seem. Some of the picturesque cottages prove to be damp, draughty and squalid when you get inside, with no lighting, no water indoors, no amenities and no comfort. The plain fact is that here in Madron there are cottages still inhabited (and by families that include children) that should have been pulled down years ago.

'Now at last, something really substantial has been achieved. In addition to the 8 new Swedish houses completed in 1947, 34 new permanent houses are nearing completion. In fact, Madron, a small village that is the centre of a comparatively small population, has had no less than 42 new houses since the end of the war. In addition the Madron water supply is receiving attention and work is well forward with a scheme that should end our water shortage for good and all. This scheme will also be completed in March.'

Left: Mrs Gendle outside Bosvean, then the Post Office, in the early 1930s

Right: 'The Reading Room' or outside privy – quaintness had its price

Below: These houses in Old Fore Street, opposite the Chapel, were pulled down to make way for bungalows

The vicar very probably had the two long terraces of cottages – Vingoe's Row and Hillside Row – in mind when he talked of ripe subjects for demolition. These were in fact pulled down in the late 1940s as the first council houses on Chapel Field, renamed Trelawny Estate, were going up.

Parc Abnac Estate was also built, in the late 50s, on land adjoining Mount View. By 1963, 86 new council houses had been provided in Madron and further development proposals came in for fierce opposition in some quarters. It was at this time that one of several 'take over bids' was floated, with the objective of enlarging Penzance's boundaries at the expense of Madron. The parish council's objection to this was well put:

> The village of Madron is separated from the Borough of Penzance by a belt of agricultural land of about half a mile and the Town and Country Planning Committee have resisted the linking of Penzance with Madron by residential or industrial development.
>
> During the post-war period the District Council has built 80 council houses in the village and also constructed 12 old people's bungalows and provided a resident warden.
>
> In view of the amenities in the village and the organisations using them, it is this council's firm opinion that the Parish of Madron should remain as heretofore a self-contained independent rural unit.
>
> To suggest divorcing the village of Madron from the large rural area in the south and north-west of the village would leave that area without a religious centre, namely the Parish Church, with its traditional links with Madron Well and Baptistry. Frankly there seems to be little point in transferring a few hundred people from one authority to another, thus destroying the cohesion of a well-organised rural community.

This put paid to any idea of encroachment and thus the matter has rested till the present day.

Development in the village continued, however. In the late 1980s the Devon and Cornwall Housing Association began to plan new housing in the Aldreath Road area. By 1992 proposals settled at 18 houses to be built, 13 of which were to be available for rent, five to be part owned. It is here that the names of the two demolished rows of cottages are perpetuated in 'Vingoe's Lane' and 'Hillside Parc'.

Few private houses were built in Madron until the 1960s when some bungalows were put up. Later, development in Churchtown came when Landithy Farm barns were converted, and most recently, in 2000, Church Way filled the remaining space.

The workmen who built Landithy Hall, which opened in 1909

Landithy Hall

Not only is this handsome hall, with its adjacent cottages in similar style, charming to the eye (a well proportioned granite façade in a graceful curve within attractive gardens), since its opening in 1909 it has been invaluable as the supreme centre for village social occasions.

Behind the hall there used to be a rifle range used by army cadets to practise firing, but eventually it fell into disrepair and was used for storage. In addition to the main hall there were three community rooms: a darts room (now the kitchen); a reading room, to which the daily papers came in the early days and young ladies of teenage years could spend quiet hours reading twice a week; and a fully equipped billiards room. Nowadays in the Forget Me Not Room villagers meet for coffee and a chat.

During the Second World War there was table tennis at the hall and fond memories are still invoked of the land girls billetted at Poltair who came up to Landithy to play ping pong.

When the hall was first built, the cottage to the left of the main door was designated for the caretaker. Those mentioned are Mr Moran (pre-war), Mr & Mrs

Landithy Hall

Allen, Mr & Mrs Eddy, then Walter Nicholls who retired to Heamoor. The cottage on the right was used by the district nurses – nurse Noble pre-war and nurse Varcoe (later Nicholls) who kept her car in the disused rifle range. In the open space behind the hall there was a tennis court, accessed by a little track between the cottages.

By 1995 it was found that renovations were advisable. An appeal was launched and a design for improvements drawn up by local chartered architect Mr CJ Rolfe. Where the rifle range had been, a passageway was made behind the stage, giving access to each side of it. The comprehensive renovations have made a centre of continuing pride whose excellent day to day condition and marvellous garden are the result of dedicated work by the present caretaker Martin Easley and his wife Val.

Final word

Madron's Story within these covers is now finished. Looking back on it and reflecting a moment, a reader might agree that it has been a long, complex and colourful tale, ever changing and rich in its centuries-old variety; a story well worth the telling and well worth the knowing.

One clear impression left by those descriptions of life in Madron which are still within the memory of our older folk is of a strong and vibrant community spirit. The pre- and post-war days were surely a golden age in the number and variety of organisations within the village from which nearly everybody derived their principal entertainment and interest. Self-sufficiency was strong, the natural leaders gave generously of their time and resources, and the people joined in wholeheartedly.

From glancing at the past it is quite natural to turn to the present and the future and perhaps to learn a lesson or two from days gone by. Those who love Madron will have a healthy concern about the parish today when it is often said that country life is under seige. But in those things which lie within the power of us ordinary villagers to influence, Madron gives every sign of good health. There are still many well supported clubs, societies and organisations flourishing, too many to list, and so long as this 'social involvement' remains strong the outlook is optimistic. If we use our school, our church, chapel, pub and shop and support our community life as well as we are able, we are doing all we reasonably can to ensure that Madron's future will be as lively as its past has been.

Index of personal and local place names